A SAVVY
CHRISTIAN'S
GUIDE TO LIFE

TRACEY D. LAWRENCE

Published by
THOMAS NELSON
Since 1798

www.thomasnelson.com

www.thomasnelson.com

Cover Design: The Designworks Group | Paul Nielsen
Interior Design: Kimberly Sagmiller, VisibillityCreative.com

ISBN 10: 1-5914-5512-X
ISBN 13: 978-1-59145-512-7

Printed in the USA

DEDICATION

THIS BOOK IS DEDICATED TO MY SAVVY FRIEND, TARA PLOG,
WHO FAITHFULLY PRAYED FOR CREATIVE ANGELS TO ATTEND ME.

TABLE OF CONTENTS

PROBLEMS WITH UNDERSTANDING GOD

PROBLEMS IN CULTURE

PROBLEMS AT WORK

PROBLEMS WITH FAMILY AND FRIENDS

FOREWORD

My son, keep my words, and treasure my commands within you.
Keep my commands and live, and my law as the apple of your eye.
Bind them on your fingers; Write them on the tablet of your heart.
Say to wisdom, "You *are* my sister," and call understanding *your*
nearest kin. Proverbs 7:1-4

Wouldn't it be nice if we had a tour guide for life that would shadow our steps, offering survival tips and sagely wisdom for those moments when we are unsure how to live out our faith? We have knowledge about our faith and inklings of what to do, but maybe just need a little more sure footing before stepping out. When do we assert our beliefs with a coworker? How do we talk to a rebellious teen? What social skills are needed to respond respectfully to a nonbeliever? Christians often find their worldview clashes with others around them, and discerning a wise and effective solution can seem impossible. Life's problems can leave us unsure about what to think, how to act, and when to speak.

The Savvy Christian's Guide to Life is a creative tutorial to help you when you need just a little more information on a topic to practically respond to life's dilemmas. As Christians, we are called to live by our convictions, not just verbalize them. But certain situations can be complicated and sometimes we may require a little help jumpstarting our brain. You may be one who is very familiar with the Bible, but aren't sure how to go about finding the passages that can help solve real life problems. Or, maybe you feel you just need a few resources from seasoned experts on a certain topic to coach you along. There is no worldview on the planet other than Christianity that gives us practical tools to live by that actually work out in real life. This handbook is designed to serve as a source of encouragement to you asserting that, Yes, it is possible to live as a disciple in the twenty-first century.

Tracey D. Lawrence

PROBLEMS WITH UNDERSTANDING GOD

Jesus said to him, "I am the way, the truth, and the life. No one comes to the Father except through Me."
John 14:6

1.

HOW CAN I BE SURE I'M WORSHIPPING THE ONE TRUE GOD?

Real Life Question:

How can I be sure I'm worshipping the One True God? Is God also Allah? And what about other good religious figures?

Life in a pluralistic society can be confusing. Our worship experience can be reduced down to style and preference rather than centered around who God really is. Christians are bombarded with the postmodern mantra, "truth is relative." This can definitely influence our thinking and make us wonder if we really have a corner on truth and if our God is really the only way.

Real Life Case Study:

Wayne is a smart, honest guy and known by his friends as being a good listener and a loyal friend. Recently, he has gone through a rough custody battle with his ex-wife and wants to give his son all he can in life. Questions about God have surfaced and so he turns to childhood friend, Sara, whom he respects.

"Sara, I'm thinking of looking for a church . . . I know you believe that Jesus is the only way, and you are the only Christian I know who actually lives out what you believe. Most Christians are too narrow-minded in my opinion, so I want to be open to other faiths."

"Wayne, thanks for the gracious compliment. I know I don't always make the right choices, but I do believe the Christian worldview is the only one that answers the hard questions about life."

"Well, I wanted to tell you I visited a Unitarian church nearby my house. I decided to attend a small group to see what the people are like. It was really great. The idea of the small groups is to learn other religious traditions of others over supper at someone's house. So we took time to pray, but it was generic enough where no one felt uncomfortable. You could pray to Jesus, Allah, Buddha, or whatever God you are comfortable with. . . . What do you think about that?"

"I'm glad you have a hunger to find truth, Wayne. Sure, I wish you would consider finding a Christian church because I honestly believe there is only One God. It's not terribly popular to assert that. But I also think you find elements of God's truth in other religions. No matter where we go, I don't think anyone can escape encountering God's truth."

"Sara, that is why I respect you. You never think I'm stupid. I'll let you know how I like the worship service, and I'd like to talk to you about it afterwards. You know, I don't want to lead my son in the wrong direction, and I do think we all have a spiritual nature that needs to be nourished. I know, whoever God is, knows that I've tried to fill it with sex and other things that haven't made life worth living as of yet."

9

"Wayne, you know I love our conversations and would love to talk to you about the church service.... By the way, have you ever noticed how we talk about God almost every time we talk? It seems I talk about God more with you than my Christian friends. I'll be praying for you."

1. Do you have a "Wayne" in your life? How has she or he helped to challenge you to solidify what you believe?

2. Have you found yourself wondering if you might be wrong about who Jesus is and that maybe the rest of the world is right?

3. If you were Sara, would you have been more assertive about Christianity? Why or why not?

4. Write out the essentials you believe about Christianity. What do you believe to be true about orthodox Christianity? Who is God and why do you believe that Jesus is the only way?

5. Read Matthew 16:13-15. Why do you think Jesus wanted the disciples to answer His question, "Who do you say that I am?"

Real Life Lessons:

If most of us are honest, we have had doubts at some point that maybe the rest of the world is right, and we are wrong about Christianity. But hopefully those doubts have led toward a deeper desire to know God and His truth, and even test it out in day-to-day living.

According to the pollsters, almost everyone believes in an ultimate power. But our views of God differ significantly, putting us in different camps. For some, God is nothing more than Mother Nature. Twelve-steppers think of God as a "Higher Power." Some believe they are evolving to be godlike. Still others are disciples of Islam. Certain views about God have generated many different paths. For the Church of Jesus Christ of Latter-Day Saints, God is a perfect exalted man with a literal flesh and bones body, but Jesus was not God. For the Christian Scientist, God is eternal, impersonal. God is viewed as spirit, not matter, therefore denying the humanity of Jesus. For the disciple of Islam, God is a tyrant and only works can save you.

The Christian believes in a personal God who came to remove the gap sin created so that we might be restored to the relationship with God we were created to have before the Fall of humanity. Nothing we do can pay that debt we owe to God, and Jesus came so that we could have eternal life with the One True God.

To be sure we are worshiping the One True God, we can take a look at the history of the church and what has been accepted as true through her existence. The Nicene Creed is the oldest theological statement of the church and most pervasive in acceptance, which affirms, among other things, the Trinity, the deity and humanity of Jesus Christ, and the personal reality of the Holy Spirit. The Apostles' Creed is also recognized throughout orthodox Christianity as tenets of our faith. These creeds came into existence to protect the true doctrine of the church and to fight heresy.

The biblical view of who God is, is not easily expressed in a short definition. As Christians, we appeal to the authority of Scripture and the body of Christ for clarity about who God is. We also

11

learn about God through nature and observable truth around us. What many other religions don't tackle is the problem of sin. Most nonbelievers don't deny there is sin in the world and that they have made wrong choices. It's pretty hard to deny the existence of evil. Christianity is the only faith that offers a solution in how to deal with sin and how to have a real relationship with the One True God.

We know, according to Scripture, that no one can be saved except through Christ. Within our limited view, it can seem that God is cruel and full of ego to expect for all to find this narrow road. But the Bible does assure us that God loves us, everyone. He wills for no one to be lost and wants all to be saved (Matthew 18:14).

Real Life Strategies:
• When looking for a church home, read their statement of faith. Ask yourself if you can adhere to their assertions.

• Develop a strong Christology. Study about who Jesus claimed to be in the Bible. (see John 1:1; Isaiah 6:1-10; John 12:37-43; John 8:24; John 8:58; John 10:30; 1 Timothy 2:5; Matthew 14:33; Revelation 5:11-14)

• If you have doubts, ask teachers and leaders you respect within your church about God.

Real Life Wisdom:
I am trying here to prevent anyone saying the really foolish thing that people often say about Him: "I'm ready to accept Jesus as a great moral teacher, but I don't accept His claim to be God." That is one thing we must not say. A man who was merely a man and said the sort of thing Jesus said would not be a great moral teacher. He would

either be a lunatic—on a level with the man who says He is a poached egg—or else He would be the Devil of Hell. You must make your choice. Either this man was, and is, the Son of God: or else a madman or something worse. You can shut Him up for a fool, you can spit at Him and kill Him as a demon or you can fall at his feet and call Him Lord and God. But let us not come with any patronizing nonsense about His being a great human teacher. He has not left that open to us. He did not intend to. —C.S. Lewis

Savvy Resources for Additional Study:
Read some of the historic creeds of Christianity:
Nicene Creed
Apostles' Creed

Study some of God's Attributes:

Psalm 139:7-10	1 John 3:20
Jeremiah 23:23-24	John 1:18
1 Kings 8:27	1 Timothy 6:16
Acts 17:24-25	Isaiah 6:3
Job 41:11	Psalm 99:9
Psalm 50:10-12	Leviticus 19:2
Revelation 19:6	Romans 16:27
Matthew 19:26	Isaiah 48:11
Ephesians 3:20	Romans 8:28
Psalm 90:2	Galatians 2:20
Revelation 1:8	John 3:16
John 4:24	

**These things
I have spoken
to you, that in
Me you may
have peace.
In the world
you will have
tribulation;
but be of good
cheer, I have
overcome the
world.** John 16:33

2.

WHY DO "GOOD" PEOPLE SUFFER?

Real Life Question:

Why does it seem like good people suffer more than bad people sometimes?

"Why do the good suffer?" has always been a difficult question throughout the history of humanity. There is something inherent in us that wants justice to be done at the end of the day. How do we trust that God is loving when there seem to be injustices around those who fear God and what appears to be no reward for suffering?

Real Life Case Study:

Brenda came to the ladies' prayer group early to talk with Pam alone. It had been a rough year in every way. She took off her hat and gave a deep sigh. Her hair was almost all grown back after surviving six months of chemotherapy.

"I can't believe this is happening to us again. Sometimes, I think

God is really out to get us. Do you know Roger has had eight different jobs in the past three years? I would almost rather go through chemo again than struggle with money again."

"I'm so sorry to hear that Roger lost his job again. We will be sure and pray for God's lead in what is next for him."

"Pam, do you think we are a target for disaster?"

Life can bring some very unexpected blows without a moment's notice. One of the hardest issues to work out in our minds is how God can allow good people to suffer.

After becoming a Christian, it doesn't take long to realize we don't live a charmed life. Suffering is no respecter of age, race, social status, or position. God is well acquainted with all of the details of our lives, though at times it may honestly feel like He isn't giving us the care and protection we want.

What do we tell our friends who are struggling with "why me?" again?

1. When you encounter suffering, what is your first reaction?

2. Think about a particularly painful trial that you persevered through. What did you learn about God that you might have not known any other way?

3. Read James 1:1-5. Reflect on James' words in light of your own experience. When has it been particularly difficult to persevere through a trial?

Real Life Lessons:

Seeing our family or good friends suffer is one of life's greatest dilemmas. Words of comfort are often inadequate and prayers can feel ineffective. How do we look at it from God's perspective? Why does the deadbeat husband who doesn't pay child support get the job promotion he's been wanting, and the faithful husband loses his job?

Looking at suffering from a Christian worldview can help. We can take heart and know that our suffering is not in vain. God does work all things for the good of those who love Him (Romans 8:28). Sometimes, we can forget the reality that we all live in a fallen world and sin has affected every generation. We cannot fully escape evil or the effects of the Fall in this life no matter what we do or where we are. Sin isn't a terribly popular doctrine, and it is easy to forget it has direct consequences on our daily lives.

This reality doesn't necessarily comfort those who need comfort from the Body of Christ, but knowing why we suffer can help the confusion in our mind. Sometimes we suffer because of our choices. When we give in to a temptation, usually there are natural consequences that cause hardship. But sometimes we suffer just because we are alive in this world. Jesus said, "He makes His sun rise on the evil and on the good, and sends rain on the just and on the unjust" (Matthew 5:45).

Take Brenda as an example. She is a Christian who is trying to serve God in the midst of hardship. Even if Brenda never committed another sin for the rest of her life, she still could not escape suffering because sin has entered this world and it affects everyone. We are promised in Scripture that we would encounter hardships and suffering.

Discerning why we suffer can be tricky. We can identify suffering occurs in three different ways: 1) We suffer by another person's sinful choices; 2) We suffer because of our own sinful choices; 3) We suffer because we cannot escape the effects of the Fall that are evident around us.

Whether or not God is pruning us through a hardship or we are suffering at the hand of another, a Christian has the promise that God is using it for good. The hard part is we might not see the evidence of the good He is working out until much later. Jesus tells Peter that Satan has asked Him if he could sift him like wheat, just as Job was tested (see Luke 22:31). Satan still seems to want to test those that call themselves disciples, and God may mysteriously allow such testing in our lives. Jesus told Peter, "But I have prayed for you." Through the testing, we have the promise of being strengthened by Jesus who intercedes for us.

We know just by experience that no one really escapes suffering, but sometimes it almost seems like the good suffer more. The Bible soberly reminds us that there is not one that is righteous; therefore we all deserve death. But God in His mercy gives us life, and we have the promise that nothing can separate us from His love. Absolutely nothing.

"Therefore let those who suffer according to the will of God commit their souls *to Him* in doing good, as to a faithful Creator" (1 Peter 4:19).

Real Life Strategies:
• Prayerfully discern the source of your suffering. Do you believe God might be building your character? Have you made some poor choices?

• Stay committed to sharing your struggles with other Christians who can give you encouragement and hope.

• If you are in a position to encourage another who is facing severe hardship, be sure to listen intently, and most of all, your goal is to point them toward God and His wisdom, not just your own.

• Be comfortable with not having an answer. If you are unsure as to what to say, remember being there for a friend is much more powerful than what we say.

Real Life Wisdom:

I have learned two lessons in my life: first, there are no sufficient literary, psychological, or historical answers to human tragedy, only moral ones. Second, just as despair can come to one another only from other human beings, hope, too, can be given to one only by other human beings. –Elie Wiesel

The world is full of suffering, it is also full of overcoming it.– Helen Keller

Savvy Resources for Additional Study:
Pick a biography to read of someone who greatly suffered for their faith for new insights on what God can do through trials and testing (i.e. Corrie Ten Boom, Dietrich Bonhoeffer, Amy Carmichael).

Read the book of Job.

And let us consider one another in order to stir up love and good works, not forsaking the assembling of ourselves together, as is the manner of some, but exhorting one another, and so much the more as you see the Day approaching.
Hebrews 10:24-25

3.
DO I REALLY HAVE TO GO TO CHURCH?

Real Life Question:

Why does God want me to keep going to church when Christians can't seem to get along? Am I supposed to put up with hypocrisy?

Unfortunately, church can be the last place we want to be sometimes. People can be the biggest stumbling block of all. When Sunday rolls around, it can be very tempting to make your altar at your bedside to avoid people.

Real Life Case Study:

Jeff grew up in a Christian home, but had strayed away from his faith as he approached college. He found himself listening to some of his humanistic professors who boldly lashed out at Christianity. Jeff assumed they knew more than he did and began to feel persuaded by the skeptical view of Christianity that permeated the campus. *How can the God of the Bible be love when*

Christians are so divided? Why do Christians say they believe one thing, then do another?

As he began to reflect on his church life, he began to recall all the ways his church had failed him. He remembered the time he invited his friend Mike to a youth event, but the youth pastor never reached out to Jeff's skeptical friend enough to make him want to come back. Then he remembered how an elder divorced his beautiful wife of twenty years and left her for a younger woman who sang in the choir. He remembers his dad coming home weary from church meetings and it seemed the leadership couldn't agree on anything. Jeff decided it was time to be honest with himself. He didn't like church, and he didn't like the Christians he encountered.

1. Most everyone has been disappointed by a Christian friend or a leader. Think about a time where you were deeply hurt by a believer whom you trusted. How did you handle the situation?

2. Read Genesis 1:27 and Psalm 8:4-9. How should we view people in light of what Scripture tells us?

3. How do you think we should treat hypocrites?

Real Life Lessons:
People, whether they are Christians or not, will inevitably fail us. The problem is we have higher expectations for those who claim to have a personal relationship with God. This isn't wrong to expect more from those who should know better, but the reality is people still sin.

Unfortunately many ex-churchgoers claim the people drove them away. Our natural inclination is to look at the people, instead of God, and get confused along the way.

Hypocrisy is a real problem in the church today, but the answer is not to abandon the church or to keep looking for the perfect church. Though our churches are terribly flawed and fragmented, Christ wants us to love His church until He returns. As the old adage says, "you can't pick your family." We are sort of stuck with each other. No matter how many churches we try, we will always find there to be hypocritical behavior. We are much better sizing up another's brand of Christianity than taking time to examine our own hearts.

Self-examination doesn't mean that we ignore the wrong behaviors we encounter around us. There are godly ways in which we are called to deal with those who sin against us (see Matthew 18). At times we are tempted to say, "It's no use to talk to her about how she gossips, so I just ignore it." God may be calling you to confront a person so that your church might be a safer, healthier place to worship Christ.

Though we gather with just common sinners each Sunday, there is a mysterious strengthening that occurs in corporate worship. The Apostle Paul said, "Now, therefore, you are no longer strangers and foreigners, but fellow citizens with the saints and members of the household of God, having been built on the foundation of the apostles and prophets, Jesus Christ Himself being the chief cornerstone, in whom the whole building, being fitted together, grows into a holy temple in the Lord, in whom you also are being built together for a dwelling place of God in the Spirit. (Ephesians 2:19-22)

21

Real Life Strategies:

• Keep your eyes focused on God, not on your personal disappointments with people.

• Be mindful of the forgiveness God has extended to you over and again. Remember that you also have disappointed someone you care about.

• Prayerfully ask God if He might be calling you to confront someone who has offended you.

Real Life Wisdom:

Through His Church, spread out around the world, Jesus is glorifying Himself and extending His reign in ways that no single person, congregation, or denomination could do alone. –Josh Harris

Savvy Resources for Additional Study:
Stop Dating the Church: Fall in Love with the Family of God
By Joshua Harris (Sisters, OR: Multnomah, 2004)

Knowing God
By J. I. Packer (Downers Grove, IL: InterVarsity, 1993)

Marks of a Healthy Church
By Mark Dever (Wheaton, IL: Crossway Books, 1997)

For the word of God is living and powerful, and sharper than any two-edged sword, piercing even to the division of soul and spirit, and of joints and marrow, and is a discerner of the thoughts and intents of the heart. Hebrews 4:12

4.
HOW CAN I UNDERSTAND THE BIBLE?

Real Life Question:

Can I really understand what the Bible has to say, and is it relevant for my life?

In our postmodern world, absolute truth has been challenged by academia, media, and pop culture; therefore, the truth contained in the Bible has also been questioned. Many Christians are left wondering, is the Bible really God's truth and can it honestly be understood by anyone thousands of years removed from the original author?

Real Life Case Study:

Kate just became a Christian and is not from a Christian home. A friend of hers invited her to youth camp. She claimed to be an atheist before that life-altering week. Kate is a deep thinker, and intellect, and a proud skeptic. But one night after the last big campfire, she asked to meet with a counselor. She knew she didn't completely understand everything she heard from the Bible that week, but had to find out more. College was to start in a few weeks, and she felt like was drifting. She knew her life and her thoughts just left her empty and in despair. But when she heard Jesus' words for the first time, hope entered the picture.

"Jen, this has been one wild week for me. I know you and I come from different worlds. Your family loves you. Well, I guess mine love me, but they also loved the benefits of sending me to boarding school all my life. ... Anyway, I felt like people here this week really were genuine and really love this Jesus whom I all of a sudden chose to follow. The counselor gave me a few chapters in John to read. I'm going to do it, but I'm just confused. How can we really know what the Bible says is true, and it is even relevant to the twenty-first century world?"

"Kate, I'm no Bible expert, but I do know when I read it, I find comfort. I somehow find help in making decisions and living out my faith. I'm not always faithful to work through the stuff I don't understand, but it really is an amazing book."

1. What has been your experience in reading the Bible? Do you feel it is mostly difficult to understand or mostly easy to understand?

2. Do you avoid verses you don't understand, or do you try and study them until you have better insight?

3. Read 2 Timothy 4:1-5. How has God's Word allowed you to "be prepared in season and out of season"?

4. Read Acts 3:21-24; Acts 28:25-27; 2 Peter 1:20-21. What did the apostles believe about the inspiration of the Old

Testament? Read 1 Corinthians 14:37. How does Paul view the letter he is writing to the church?

Real Life Lessons:

The relevancy of the Bible has been challenged in our culture and even in the church. Some pastors have even taken the approach on Sundays to refer to a Bible passage, but not require anyone to look at the text, which can leave visitors questioning if the Bible really is all that important today. A cultural lie we hear today is, "The Bible is an old book from a different culture, so it is impossible to take it seriously in the modern world." What is so stunning about the Bible is that it has transcended time, race, and all classes of people for thousands of years and still is God's story of reconciliation to His people—a message for all generations. This book is unique among all documents of ancient literature. Composed over a 1500-year time span using forty human authors, it stands alone in literature by its character, . assertions, consistency, attestations, and usage.

God has revealed Himself to us in two distinct ways. Theologians refer to them as general revelation and special revelation. Special revelation is contained in the pages of Scripture. General revelation contains all the other ways we can know about God. The Bible reveals to us specific information that is for the benefit of our relationship with God. It is all about being reconciled to God. We can understand this process better by being a student of the Bible.

It is helpful to have a little bit of knowledge about hermeneutics—how to interpret the Bible. Part of the reason we have such a challenge to see Scripture's relevance in our daily lives is because of the postmodern view that truth depends on what works for an individual, not on authority. But for orthodox Christianity, the Bible has always carried authority throughout history. As Christians, we begin with the premise that the Bible is God's word to humanity.

Even though Christians believe in the reliability and authority of Scripture, interpreting its meaning can lead to disagreement among Christians. We can look at various denominations within Christendom and see that we all don't agree on everything, such as predestination, baptism, the Second Coming, and many other issues. Though we may disagree on certain passages through Scripture, we can agree that through the Bible God equipped His people to serve His purposes and it is sufficient for us to live out our Christian faith. We are given a structure of who God is, a guide to worship, the mission of the church, how to conduct our daily lives, rebuke and promise from God's prophets, praise and lament, and a future hope. We can rely on what we have in the Bible to accurately reveal the story of God. But it is important to also realize that though the Bible is inspired and authoritative, it is also limited. Think in terms of the incarnation. Jesus gave up His throne to take on flesh as a man, therefore, limited Himself. He still had authority and was still God, but was limited by His humanity during His earthly ministry. The same is true regarding the Bible. Though it is authoritative, it is also limited by human words and language. The Bible is God's revelation to humanity, but He does speak in other ways as well (i.e. through Creation, through people, through His Spirit).

It helps to be sensitive to the different genres of writing within Scripture that you will encounter. For example, you don't view the Psalms exactly the way you would view Genesis. Genesis is a narrative, and the book of Psalms is full of poetry and the prayers of God's people. Further, Revelation and Daniel contain apocalyptic literature which is highly symbolic and can be difficult to understand, and shouldn't be read as literally as other books. Not all of the Bible can be read devotionally. Some of the Bible is a record of history and informative about the past. So get to know the authors. Buy a commentary and a concordance. Learn the different genres and the history of the Christian Bible. You will be able to conclude firsthand that all we have in Scripture is reliable and God-breathed (2 Timothy 3:16).

Real Life Strategies:

- The Bible is useful for teaching, rebuking, correcting, and training.

- The Bible equips us for every good work (2 Timothy 3:17)

- Study Scripture with other Christians to sharpen your interpreting skills. We need the authority of the church to keep us on track.

- Scripture should be interpreted in light of Scripture and in the whole context of God's nature.

- Take time to study how the canon of Scripture came about.

Real Life Wisdom:

The Bible is the cradle wherein Christ was laid. –Martin Luther

And the words of the LORD are pure words, like silver tried in a furnace of earth, purified seven times. —Psalm 12:6

Savvy Resources for Additional Study:

Study the active nature of God's word: Ephesians 6:17; Matthew 4:1-11; Ephesians 5:25-26; John 15:3; John 17:17; 1 Peter 1:23; James 1:21; Romans 15:4; 1 Peter 1:24-25; Acts 8:26-35; Romans 10:17. Write out your findings.

Psalm 119 is one of the most powerful passages in the Bible about God's Word. This is also the longest chapter in the Bible. Sometime this week make a list of the benefits of God's Word as a reminder to you of the relevance Scripture has in our lives. List also the misfortunes mentioned to those who reject it.

The Last Word by N.T. Wright

And there shall be no more curse, but the throne of God and of the Lamb shall be in it, and His servants shall serve Him. They shall see His face, and His name shall be on their foreheads. There shall be no night there: They need no lamp nor light of the sun, for the Lord God gives them light. And they shall reign forever and ever.
Revelation 22:3-5

5.
WHAT CAN I KNOW ABOUT HEAVEN?

Real Life Question:

Do I really have anything to look forward to in the next life, and does Heaven make sense of the life I've lived here?

I feel like I've messed up this life quite a bit and haven't had the best family or set of circumstances to deal with. What can I really know about Heaven, and what difference does it make?

Real Life Case Study:

Joe just celebrated his fiftieth wedding anniversary. All six children and their fifteen grandchildren were able to come for the celebration. The food, fellowship, and slide show were enjoyed by all 200 people who attended. Life had been good to Joe and Mary.

Joe had a moment to talk with his oldest son, Chris, after a wild, long photo session with the family.

"Dad, you should be proud of all you've done to be a good father and husband. I know God is going to reward your faithfulness to him."

"You know, son, I haven't given much thought to Heaven. Life has been so good to me here. I feel in some ways I've already experienced Heaven. I guess I don't like to think about Heaven and maybe haven't come to grips with the reality that it may be near. I'm so busy, I guess I just haven't had a need to think about it."

"Yeah, well. I guess I feel like I've experienced more of Hell here on earth than Heaven. I've made a mess of my life and I know my kids are paying for my choices. I just keep wondering, does my life here connect with what is in store for me in Heaven? Does my tangled past with God still hold promise to a better day with Him?"

All of us question what Heaven will be like at one time or another. Maybe you resonate with Joe. Maybe you resonate with Chris. Some might worry that Heaven only promises harp lessons and cloud sitting with angels. Others might worry that they might be second class citizens in Heaven because of the sins they committed on Earth. What difference does Heaven make to me now? Are our lives forgotten here and everything goes down the drain, or do all the questions about life finally get tied together? The truth remains that God is at work preparing a place for us, where our lives will be lived to the fullest.

1. What are some of your hopes about Heaven? Your fears?

2. List some of the impressions you have about life in Heaven. Refer to what you know Scripture reveals about Heaven.

3. Do you think we have lost the hope of Heaven? If so, why do you think our church culture has forgotten what we are promised?

4. Read 2 Peter 3:13; Hebrews 1:10-12; Revelation 21:1; Revelation 21:3; Ephesians 1:10. Record what these passages tell us about Heaven.

Real Life Lessons:

All of humanity was created to live in eternal fellowship with our Creator. This fellowship was broken at the Fall of man, and God has been working ever since to reconcile us back to Himself. As Christians we have confidence about what we face in death because we are confident life's road leads somewhere—our final home. But we don't act too jazzed about the real hope we really have. Unfortunately our mental pictures of Heaven don't seem to move us, as we think of sappy, syrupy, even dull images about our final destination. If we keep such notions about Heaven, we are robbing ourselves of knowing more about one of the most fascinating doctrines of Christianity.

Typically a lot of us postmodern Christians feel bored, cynical, and burnt out. Technology has robbed us a lot of richness our faith has to offer because we are so preoccupied with information overload. Every moment of the day, our culture is trying to fill it with thoughts on how to be happy here and now, leading us to believe that only now matters. But as Christians much of our hope lies in the future, and the Bible has a lot to say about what is to come. We know that all roads don't lead to Heaven; we are dependent on the saving work of Christ. He is the One who gives this life meaning and connects us to the next. The last thing the devil wants us to believe is that we really do have a future and hope. Everything we endure here will one day make sense when we dwell with our Creator forever.

The Bible is clear: Everything is better in Heaven. Worship, work, and relationships move toward an ultimate fullness that we have yet to know. "Eye has not seen, nor ear heard, nor have entered into the heart of man the things which God has prepared for those who love Him " (1 Corinthians 2:9).

We have an innate need to know that our life matters for something. Rick Warren, in his book The Purpose Driven Life, struck a chord with humanity—does anything I do really matter? Many believers and nonbelievers have been challenged to live with greater purpose because of the reminder that God's reality says our lives are destined to be great. Theologian Peter Kreeft says it this way: "My greatness depends on reality's greatness. If reality does not extend to Heaven, I cannot either. Even if I am a small fish, I am greater if I am a small fish in a big reality-pond than if I am a big fish in a small reality-pond. That is why C.S. Lewis makes the surprising judgment that 'it is more important that heaven should exist than that any of us should reach it.'"[a]

Our deepest need is for reality, and to ignore the reality of Heaven in this life is to leave it empty. Imagine every life experience, every joy, sorry, frustration, failure, pleasure, and tragedy all coming together and making one indescribable life with God Himself and His family. The best is yet to come, and God wants us to start living like we know that.

Real Life Strategies:

• Remember your life matters now because you are closer and closer to the hope of Heaven.

• Don't get to the extreme of wasting your life now because you are too preoccupied with Heaven. Suicide is not an option. We are never to abandon the assignments and meaningful work we are to do here and now for His kingdom.

• The natural tendency is to separate divine things and earthly things. They go together and are not opposite worlds. Remember Christ shows us the cooperation of Earth and Heaven coming together through His incarnation. Live like you believe this truth.

Real Life Wisdom:

The best life on earth is a glimpse of Heaven; the worst of life is a glimpse of Hell. For Christians, this present life is the closest they will ever come to Hell. For the unbelievers, it is the closest they will come the Heaven. –Randy Alcorn

Savvy Resources for Additional Study:
Everything You Ever Wanted to Know About Heaven ... But Never Dreamed of Asking
by Peter Kreeft (Ignatius Press: San Francisco, 1990)

Heaven by Randy Alcorn (Tyndale: Grand Rapids, 2004)

Read about what worship in heaven is like: Revelation 1:6; 4:4, 9-11; Revelation 5:8-10, 13; 7:12.

(Endnotes)

a   Peter Kreeft, *Everything You Ever Wanted to Know about Heaven* (Ignatius Press: San Franciso, 1990)

33

For I know that in me (that is, in my flesh) nothing good dwells; for to will is present with me, but how to perform what is good I do not find. For the good that I will to do, I do not do; but the evil I will not to do, that I practice.
Romans 7:18-19

6.
HOW CAN I BE A SINNER AND A SAINT AT THE SAME TIME?

Real Life Question:

Why do I knowingly sin when I know God's will is always the better way than following my bad choices?

Everyone is tempted to sin though God has undeniably saved us. The Christian has the assurance that nothing separates us from God. Yet as we go about our day, we find many other voices and influences bidding us to follow what the world says is right. Sometimes it is hard to believe that we are holy when we still find we struggle with sin.

Real Life Case Study:

Steve calls David for some advice. He knew he could trust David with the really hard, raw truth about his life.

"David, thanks for making time to talk to me. I'm really struggling to do what is right."

"Well, you've been there for me as long as I can remember. Now that you are traveling more, we need to make a point to at least catch up by phone more often."

"Yeah, I think I need that. Well, since I took the new job promotion I'm always gone. Lindsey is very frustrated and really is running the house and taking care of the kids herself. I know we have really drifted apart....There is no easy way to say this ...I've been having an affair. David, please pray for me. I'm going to break it off tonight. I don't want to because I feel so lonely right now, but I also know that God is deeply grieved by this. I've been a Christian for twenty years, and I never thought that this could even happen to me."

"I'm so sorry to hear you are going through this. I'm going to be praying like crazy for you. God is going to give you the strength to break this off. You guys can make it through this. You know the Holy Spirit is at work in you, and Jesus sees you as a child of God. Don't forget that, no matter how much the guilt tries to swallow you up."

1. Think about a time when your sinful desires kept you from wanting to follow God's way. What made you finally surrender the situation over to God? Or not surrender?

2. As a Christian, do you struggle with the tension of being a sinner and yet a saint (see 2 Corinthians 5:21)?

3. Read Romans 7:13-8:1. We know that even Christians have the seed of rebellion in our hearts. When was the last incident you remember when the Holy Spirit convicted you of the goodness of the law and saved you from hurting others?

Real Life Lessons:

It's true, Christians are righteous and yet sinners at the same time. This paradox has been discussed throughout the history of Christianity. Reformer Martin Luther called this concept *Simul Justus et Peccator*—righteous and yet the same time a sinner. The believer here on earth is both completely righteous and sinful. The inspiration for this idea was taken from Luther's personal experience and from the seventh chapter of Romans. Luther's primary concern with this doctrine was the individual, but he also applied the *simul* to the Church: He said,

"God deals so wonderfully with his saints that he constantly brings it about in the Church, that the Church is holy and nevertheless not holy, that someone is righteous and at the same time not righteous, that another is blessed and at the same time not blessed."

After we become a Christian, we experience living with the tension of our righteous status (how God views us) and battling against our desire to sin. Sometimes it is easy to think of our salvation as a one-time event that gives us eternal life. But it is much more than this. Once we accept the gift of salvation, we find a relationship with God has profound blessing on all of life, but we have to keep working toward godliness with the help of His Spirit. Romans 7 deals with the struggle we face, a struggle known as sanctification. This is part of the process of being a disciple of Christ. There is disagreement within orthodox Christianity whether the process of sanctification is ever completed within the earthly lifetime of a believer. Do we ever stop sinning? We know that the sanctification process is a supernatural work of God, which rests on God ultimately. However, throughout Scripture Christians are encouraged to work at growth and maturity, which requires discipline on our part to make the right choices. The

Apostle Paul urges the practice of virtues and admonishes us to avoid evil (Romans 12:9, 16-17). The truth is that sanctification is hard, hard work.

Though it can seem hopeless at times, it is possible not to sin. We can overcome our sinful desires when we exercise discipline with the help of the Holy Spirit. Sometimes it is hard not to be discouraged when we fail, but we know Jesus has made up for our shortcomings and mistakes. Sanctification is not a passive process where we wait for the Spirit to do all the work. We are colaborers with God, and He wants our cooperation. Our holiness does not depend ever on what we do, but securely rests on God's shoulders. With that, we are not condemned when we fail and fall short, but rather we can press on toward the righteous life we were called to live.

Real Life Strategies:
- Never think you have arrived as a Christian. Always acknowledge your need for growth.

- Remember there is nothing you can do that will make God love you more than He does right now.

- Don't give up the good fight of faith. Being a Christian can be hard work. Make sure you have friends who are praying for you and concerned with your relationship with God.

Real Life Wisdom:
In efficacious grace we are not merely passive, nor yet does God do some and we do the rest. But God does all, and we do all. God produces all, we act all. For that is what produces, viz. our own acts. God is the only proper author and fountain; we only are the proper actors. We are in different respects, wholly passive and wholly active.
—Jonathan Edwards

37

Savvy Resources for Additional Study:

Read Galatians 5

Take time to read some of the great theologians of Christianity, focusing on their struggle to reconcile the paradox of being a sinner and a saint.

A Plain Account of Christian Perfection
by John Wesley (London: Epworth, 1952).
John Wesley: A Theological Journey
by Kenneth J. Collins (Abingdon Press, 2003).

Love Divine, All Loves Excelling
Words: Charles Wesley, 1747
Music: John Zundel, 1870

1. Love divine, all loves excelling, joy of heaven, to earth come down; fix in us thy humble dwelling; all thy faithful mercies crown! Jesus thou art all compassion, pure, unbounded love thou art; visit us with thy salvation; enter every trembling heart.

2. Breathe, O breathe thy loving Spirit into every troubled breast! Let us all in thee inherit; let us find that second rest. Take away our bent to sinning; Alpha and Omega be; end of faith, as its beginning, set our hearts at liberty.

3. Come, Almighty to deliver; let us all thy life receive; suddenly return and never, nevermore thy temples leave. Thee we would be always blessing, serve thee as thy hosts above, pray and praise thee without ceasing, glory in thy perfect love.

4. Finish, then, thy new creation; pure and spotless let us be. Let us see thy great salvation perfectly restored in thee; changed from glory into glory, till in heaven we take our place, till we cast our crowns before thee, lost in wonder, love, and praise.

"But that you may know that the Son of Man has power on earth to forgive sins"—He said to the man who was paralyzed, "I say to you, arise, take up your bed, and go to your house."

Luke 5:24

7.
DOES GOD STILL PERFORM MIRACLES TODAY?

Real Life Question:

Can I expect God to perform a miracle today like He did so clearly in the Bible?

Life can throw us all some hard knocks and sometimes the only answer seems to be a miracle, if only God would intervene and perform a miracle on our behalf. Sometimes the trial lingers and only grows worse and we grow more helpless. Whether we are facing severe financial hardship, terminal illness, or broken relationships, most of us have found ourselves praying for a miracle.

Real Life Case Study:

"Dear God:

You have heard my cry for help each day, and I just don't know how things got so out of hand in my family. Doug and I hardly speak anymore because we are parents sick with worry, and it is consuming us on the inside. I'm not sure how much more I can bear. I don't know if I have the strength to take Timmy to chemotherapy one more time."

"I beg You to heal him and not take him from me. The doctor says he has a matter of a few months to live, but I know You can change that prognosis and instantly heal his little body. I know You are watching over us and love us, but sometimes I don't feel You are near at all. I want to give up and just stop hoping. It hurts too much to hope."

"But something in me is still coming to You for help. Please, God, heal my son, and make him completely well. Help Doug and me trust You and have enough faith to trust You. My faith is weak right now but I ask You for a miracle. . . . Amen."

Asking God for a miracle can feel like a very vulnerable thing to do. Many times we don't feel worthy of such a display of power in our lives. We often can believe it when someone else attests to a miracle in their life, but seems much harder to believe God would move in such a way for us.

1. Describe a time in your life when you felt like the only solution was a miracle. How did God take care of you during that time? Do you feel you experienced a miracle?

2. Take time to read some of the miracles Jesus performed during His earthly ministry (Matthew 8:1-4, 14-17; Luke 7:11-17; John 2:1-11). Reflect on the different situations presented in these passages.

3. Reflect on a time you witnessed a miracle or you received one yourself. How did it affect your image of God?

4. What do you believe about miracles happening today?

Real Life Lessons:

Sometimes it is hard to discern how to pray for someone who has a terminal illness. Do we ask boldly for cancer to be gone, or do we simply plead for God's will in the situation?

Christianity has a history of miracles. Understanding the role of miracles in the spread of Christianity is an important imperative for today's Christian. Unlike today, the ancient world was not suspicious of miracles. Miracles didn't present a problem to the early Christians. A miracle is an event which runs counter to knowledge we have about nature. There are quite likely higher laws which are still unknown to us.

The miracles we encounter in the Bible have a definite purpose: to make the glory and love of God known to humanity. We've read throughout the Old and New Testaments God's saving work on behalf of His people. The parting of the Red Sea was a miracle of love, action, and deliverance for God's people. This event was celebrated and remembered by the Israelites more than any other event. God even stopped the revolution of the earth on its axis in response to Joshua's prayer (Joshua 10:12-14). Miracles remind God's people that He is working to restore all things to its proper order. A central miracle of the New Testament is the resurrection of Christ. Every book in the New Testament affirms this miracle. Belief in this miracle is essential to the orthodoxy of our faith. The Resurrection made Christian growth possible. We remember the disciples after Jesus' death—downtrodden, without hope, and defeated. But after they had witnessed the resurrected Christ, their faith grew and they powerfully spread the Gospel.

Miracles serve as signs of God's kingdom. Doctors have testified to not understanding how cancer can be in one X-ray and then gone the next day. We know that Jesus showed great compassion on the sick and even the dead during His ministry. We know He welcomes our prayers of faith that desire for a loved one to be healed in this lifetime. Sometimes we question if we should boldly pray to eradicate cancer or humbly submit to it. The tension of how to view miracles becomes more real in the realm of prayer and what we ask God for.

Miracles also serve to meet human needs. Throughout His ministry, Jesus moved about the crowds with compassion and mercy, reaching out to those hurting. He never chose to make a public display of power through miracles to serve Himself. Rather, they were to speak to God's ability to meet the needs of His people and respond to their requests.

Most of us would claim that we would welcome a miracle to change a hopeless situation. Martyrs, missionaries, and the spiritually oppressed might even believe miracles to be commonplace or the way they are able to survive in the midst of spiritual warfare. But for most Christians, our days with God take on more of the natural order with not many signs pointing us to a miraculous event. Perhaps some of this is due to our complacency. Jesus said He was unable to perform some miracles due to the lack of faith in His hometown. Somehow our faith miraculously moves God to act on our behalf. Sometimes He doesn't perform a miracle because His way is higher and better. Other times it could be simply due to our lack of faith.

Real Life Strategies:
* There is no proof that the age of miracles have ceased. Just ask any missionary.

- Miracles serve to glorify God and bring about His desired will.

- If you pray for a miracle and God does not grant your request, remember He is no less faithful than if had He performed a miracle.

Real Life Wisdom:

I think miracles exist in part as gifts and in part as clues that there is something beyond the flat world we see. –Peggy Noonan

A miracle is an event which creates faith. That is the purpose and nature of miracles. Frauds deceive. An event which creates faith does not deceive: therefore it is not a fraud, but a miracle. –George Bernard Shaw

Savvy Resources for Additional Study:
Miracles
by C.S. Lewis (New York: MacMillan. 1960)

The Heavenly Man: Brother Yun
By Paul Hattaway

Take time to read some of Jesus' miracles in the Gospels:
Jesus turning Water to Wine
Healing the Leper
Healing the Deaf and the Lame
Healing the Woman with a Blood Condition
Healing Peter's Mother-in-Law
Casting Out Demons
Raising Lazarus from the Dead
Jesus' Resurrection

> Be anxious for nothing, but in everything by prayer and supplication, with thanksgiving, let your requests be made known to God; and the peace of God, which surpasses all understanding, will guard your hearts and minds through Christ Jesus.
>
> **Philippians 4:6-7**

8.
HOW CAN I IMPROVE MY PRAYER LIFE?

Real Life Question:

How can I improve my prayer life? Sometimes I feel like my prayers are effective, and other times I feel like they don't make it past the ceiling. How do I stay motivated, no matter if I get the answers from God or not?

Prayer is one of the hardest disciplines for a Christian. It is one of those aspects of our relationship with God that is easier to talk about than to actually do. We know God answers prayer, but are more inclined to believe He would answer someone else's prayers than our own.

Real Life Case Study:

Anne has been praying for the same thing for years. Some days more fervently than others, but she doesn't seem to get much indication that God is answering. Anne has always wanted to pursue her art, and she knows it is a career choice with lots of risks and sacrifice. Some of her friends say it is obvious God is closing the doors, so move on. Anne isn't convinced, as she believes that perseverance is a part of life.

Jim, on the other hand, is amazed at God's faithfulness to answer his prayers so quickly in this season of his life. It seems before he utters a prayer, God has already intervened and done a work on his behalf. He has had a lot of tragedy in his family, but it seems like things are really turning around for him. A few months ago, Jim's mom was diagnosed with cancer, but when the doctors came out of surgery, they told the family that there was no trace to be found—truly a miracle. Jim also just received a major promotion that will really help in planning for a family. And Jim loves his work and feels a strong call to witness to his coworkers. Several have come to know the Lord, and Jim is so excited to see the attitudes change in the office.

Maybe you relate to Anne, or maybe you relate to Jim. Prayer can be such a mystery, and there seems to be many different ways that it can be approached. Sometimes when we get lots of answers, it is easier to stay motivated.

1. Think about your own prayer life. Are you satisfied with it?

2. Read through Jesus' model prayer in Matthew 6:5-14. When you pray, what do you usually focus on?

3. From what you know about Scripture and the model prayers we do have in the Bible, what do you think moves God to answers prayer?

4. A large part of Jesus' model prayer is asking God to meet our needs and even our desires. Speculate a bit as to why you think God likes us to ask Him.

5. What is the most baffling thing about prayer for you?

Real Life Lessons:

Prayer can conjure up all kinds of thoughts and feelings for Christians such as comfort, impatience, discipline, rest, anger, gratitude, despair, and hope. Prayer is simply talking to God, but we seem to get stalled out at times and not sure at all what to say. Realizing the simple nature of prayer can help us overcome our feelings of inadequacy. Mother Teresa wrote, "Prayer is simply talking to God. He speaks to us: we listen. We speak to Him: He listens. A two-way process: speaking and listening."

Mysteriously, God invites us to a dialogue with Him. The fact that the Creator of the universe wants to commune with us is unfathomable, but true. Prayers can be full of emotion or pregnant with reverent silence directed toward God in hopes He will speak. Realize that you do not have to take laborious classes on prayer to actually do it. There may be discussions about prayer that will be of benefit, but remember God does not need you to be skilled in prayer in order to start talking to Him daily.

The more time we spend with God dialoguing about our lives, the better able we will get to know our Creator. Jesus said to His disciples that it was better for Him to go away so that the Holy Spirit would come as our teacher. As we practice the discipline of prayer, we will naturally learn how to wait in silence and listen for His voice and His counsel. We are assured that He is with us when we pray.

Don't feel guilty for asking God for things in prayer. This is an important part of your relationship with your Heavenly Father. He wants to hear about all that concerns you. This is a big part of what prayer is, looking to God as your ultimate source. But even more than that, God desires to be in company with those He loves. When we take time to oblige Him, a whole new perspective flows out of us. The day takes on a meaningful shape, and you find yourself less prone to just drift, and just exist through another day. When you spend time with God, He gives you eyes to see things that you would not see otherwise. Psalm 10:4 says, "In his pride the wicked does not seek him; in all his thoughts there is no room for God" (NIV). Prayer makes room for God, giving us the godly perspective we need.

The more time you spend in prayer, the more trust you will have in God's ability to guide you. You may find yourself with impressions and thoughts that you would not have had apart from prayer and spending focused time with God. The Lord may convict you to pray for a broader scope of petitions, rather than just your immediate needs, to feel compassion for those that you would not normally apart from keeping company with God.

The book of Psalms is really a book of the Bible on the prayers of His people. As you read through them, notice the honestly in which God's followers prayed to Him. Think about your own prayers. Do you feel you are able to be honest with Him and vulnerable to be yourself? When you are more honest, you may also find that your prayers become more real and take on new life and effectiveness. Realize there is no formula to prayer, other than to make it a part of your daily life with God. He will show you what to pray when you find yourself without words. The more time you spend with God, the more you will be content to just be with Him, not really expecting anything in return, other than a growing relationship with Him. Prayer powerfully orients us to the real world, God's world.

Real Life Strategies:

● Widen your prayers beyond your comfort zone. Pray for more than your friends; pray for your enemies.

● Remember our call to pray without ceasing. Even when we are going about our day, we need to remember to open to His prompting and leading.

● Pray for big things, like the AIDS epidemic, terrorism, and even world peace. God is faithful in the big and the small.

● Prayer is not a formula, but a pursuit of a relationship.

Real Life Wisdom:

Learning to dialogue with God will never end because we are unequal partners, God and I. Admitting that, bowing before it, helps open my ears. Pursuing God despite the differences helps open my mouth, and then my heart. –Phillip Yancey

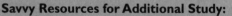

Savvy Resources for Additional Study:
Prayer for Beginners
By Peter Kreeft

Prayer
By Karl Barth (London: Westminster John Knox Press, 2002)

'The effective, fervent prayer of a righteous man avails much.'

James 5:16

9.
DOES PRAYER MAKE A DIFFERENCE?

Real Life Question:

Since God already knows all my needs, why should I pray? Does it really make a difference?

It can seem senseless to ask God, who is omniscient, telling Him what we need when He already knows. It is also easy to reason that He knows better than we do what we should have or not have, so why not just leave it up to Him rather than be disappointed when He says no.

Real Life Case Study:

Sheri and Darren's small group had just finished socializing and they realized the time had gotten away from them.

"Hey all, it's been really fun just catching up on life, but I just realized we are almost out of time. Let's take prayer requests real quick before we all head home," said Darren.

"How is everyone doing? Any special needs?" asked Sheri.

"Yes," said Myrna. "My dad has been out of work for some time and it's just hard at his age finding work. You know all the age discrimination stuff that goes on. He is just really discouraged. Please pray for him."

"I have one," said Cheryl. "Some friends of ours are in China right now getting their baby girl. I'd like to pray for safety for them and that they would bond with baby Lilly."

"You bet," said Darren. "Any others?"

"Umm . . . I just have an unmentionable. I'm just struggling with some hard stuff, so please pray for me," confessed Brian.

"Oops, well, looks like our time is up. Well, we know God knows all of our needs, so thanks for sharing your requests. We'll just try and be mindful this week to pray for each other. ... Thanks for coming. Next time we'll make time to pray together. Meanwhile, let's just send our thoughts for one another up to God."

1. Do you find that this scenario can often be true for you, you just run out of time to actually pray?

2. What are some ways you can make more effort to actually pray and not just talk about it?

3. List some reasons you can think of that would answer why God wants us to pray to Him even though He already knows our needs.

4. Read Daniel 6:10-23. How did God choose to answer Daniel's prayers? What was his commitment to prayer like?

Real Life Lessons:

One attribute that we know about God is that He is omniscient. This can pose a problem for us as we try and exercise discipline in prayer. We can get lazy and convince ourselves that we are off the hook, since He knows everything that is going on anyway. But God is clear that He wants us to pray.

Think about Jesus' model prayer. It covers just about everything— our physical needs, our relationships, and our spiritual needs. So Jesus clearly asserts to the disciples that God wants us to ask Him for what we need. This is a big part of prayer, but not all of what prayer is.

Prayer can feel stale and lifeless at times. But God is at work when we take time to exercise the discipline of prayer. He is a personal God who wants fellowship with us. Just as you might pore over the details of your day with a friend or a spouse, so we should share our heart with God. He longs for time with us, and sometimes we forget this simple truth.

There are many mysteries to prayer. We know sometimes our prayers are answered instantly. Other times we only experience frustrating silence and we wonder why ask one more time. Much of the beauty of prayer is how we are changed when we commune with God. When we spend time with our Heavenly Father, we are changed. Prayer changes the pray-er. Though prayer can feel like a monologue, it is a dynamic dialogue when we learn to listen for Him.

When we persist in prayer there is also benefit to our character. We learn how to persist, though we may be discouraged at times. Think about how Abraham, Moses, and Jacob persevered with God through honest communication. They expressed their

THE SAVVY CHRISTIAN'S GUIDE TO LIFE

doubts and frustrations and even bartered with God. Sometimes God was emotionally moved by their request and He complied. Other times He gave a deafening, resounding "no." But through wrestling with God through prayer, they were strengthened and matured in their faith.

Philip Yancey, in his book *Prayer: Does It Make Any Difference?*, says: "As I persist in prayer I recognize an answering partner who takes up the other side of the dialogue, a kind of internal alter ego representing God's point of view. When I want revenge, this partner reminds me of forgiveness; when obsessed with my own selfish needs, I am struck with the needs of others. Suddenly I realize I am not talking to myself ."

When you are feeling like prayer doesn't matter, think of the many examples we have in the Bible when God is mysteriously moved by the petition of His people, who received from God and were also changed. Of course He knows every detail of our lives, but He wants to be with us. In our busy lives, it is easier to think about prayer, even send thoughts upward to God, but never take the time to actually pray. When we take time to pray we are allowing our Heavenly Father to mold us into His likeness. Prayer is the one act that continues to bring us back together with God, declaring that we recognize we are His children.

Real Life Strategies:
● If you have not made a regular time of day to pray, make a point to do so.

● You don't have to be an expert on prayer to start talking daily to God.

● Record answers to prayer to remind you that God is faithful to move on our behalf.

● Don't let anxiety keep you from praying. Recognize this is when you need to do it most of all.

Real Life Wisdom:

We must not pray first of all because it feels good or helps, but because God loves us and wants our attention. –Henri Nouwen

Savvy Resources for Additional Study:
Prayer: Does It Make Any Difference?
By Phillip Yancey (Grand Rapids, MI: Zondervan, 2006)

The Road to Daybreak
By Henri Nouwen (New York: Doubleday, 1988)

Spiritual Disciplines
By Richard Foster

> But the hour is coming, and now is, when the true worshipers will worship the Father in spirit and truth; for the Father is seeking such to worship Him. God *is* Spirit, and those who worship Him must worship in spirit and truth.
>
> John 4:23-24

10.
HOW DO I KNOW IF I'M WORSHIPPING GOD RIGHT?

Real Life Question:

How do I know if my church is worshipping in spirit and in truth? I know that worship is more than a song, but it seems really confusing that no one agrees on what is right for the worship service.

Real Life Case Study:

Creekside Community had just experienced another significant growth spurt. The pastor was very pleased to see that they were reaching a broader demographic, but new problems did arise from the older members.

"Pastor Joe, it is just way too loud in the sanctuary. Can you give us seniors a break, please? I just don't know if my ear drums can stand it anymore."

"Mike, I'm so sorry about that. I will talk to our tech staff and see what can be done."

"That would be swell. And these praise choruses. Well, they are okay, but we sing them over and over and sometimes I feel like a broken record. Do you think you might try and offer some of the congregation a traditional service? I think that might just solve everything."

"Mike, that may work. I will talk to the elders about it. I'm just not sure logistically how we would do it. I mean we've already got a youth service going on in the gym, our regular service, and then our even louder service for the twenty-somethings. ... Well, we'll figure out something."

1. What issues are you experiencing in your church regarding worship music?

2. How do we benefit from corporate worship as the body of Christ?

3. When it comes to music and style of service, what is your preference? Do you feel our preferences should divide us into different groups on Sunday mornings? Why or why not?

4. Read 2 Peter 1:2-7. What does this passage teach us about the nature of worship?

Real Life Lessons:

Why all the controversy about worship these days? And when referring to worship, we often mean "music." Christian artists have followed the trend, devoting their latest CD projects to worship and praise music. New praise choruses are being cranked out as part of cutting edge evangelism, hoping to attract more seekers. But are we going deep enough in our Christian thought to truly understand the biblical mandate to worship?

Many postmodern Christians claim they want to experience "authentic worship." Local churches are creating hefty budgets to try and incorporate all of the arts in their weekly worship services. Not a bad idea. The church should be producing the best art and music. But sadly, however, this attempt is often rooted in a shallow understanding of worship and the arts.

In his book, *Unceasing Worship*, professor and composer Harold Best challenges the church to take another look at what it means to engage in authentic worship, exposing some bad theology we've adopted along the way. Best challenges the believer to realize worship is not a new, specialty brand of music but rather a "wonderfully complex practice." We worship while we watch the sun rise, prepare a meal for our family, or serve our boss responsibly at work. Worship never ceases. "As God eternally outpours within His triune self, and we are created in His image, it follows that we too are continuous outpourers, incurably so. …Salvation is the only way our continuous outpouring—our continuous worship—is set aright and urged into the fullness of Christ."

But many Christians are buying into the idea that authentic worship comes from a contemporary sound of music and a hip looking soloist, solemnly sharing his having a bad day in between songs. This theology fails to take into account that authentic worship is rooted in worshiping the One True God, not dependent on a musical preference or public declarations that stink sometimes.

God alone is the only authenticator of true worship.

Until we grasp the full implication that our life offered fully to God in service is a continuous outpouring, we can't really speak with authority and freedom about music and the arts. Best says, "We make and offer art because we worship; we should not make it to lead us into worship. …let's get music and the arts back where it belongs—as a lisping sign and not a glittering cause, as the response to a commandment and not just a set of tools for influencing people."

What really authenticates worship is Christ. Our common worship of Christ unites us. Yet on Sundays we find it is style of music that determines where and when we worship. This can cause Christians to be puzzled about what worship really is about. Perhaps you are one who has been confused about what worship really is. Worship is first and foremost a lifestyle and we can worship God in many ways. No doubt corporately sung music is a powerful expression of our faith and testimony. But it is just one aspect of worship that should overflow into our lives, after we leave the church building on Sunday. Worship of God should never cease once we go home.

It is easy to join in on what music is most sacred or holy. The truth is God needs every generation to sing new songs of worship and praise. But as Christians we need to be aware of the danger that music can divide, but always Christ unites. Our love for one another must far surpass our CD collections. The church should never stop singing and creating art with great reverence as an act of humble service to God, but we also must realize a thousand tongues will never be enough.

Real Life Strategies:

• If you tend to choose a service that is based on musical preference, try another service just to meet more of your church family.

• Make sure you do not succumb to chronological snobbery in the way of worship music, disregarding something as authentic because it too old, or too new. Be concerned that it doctrinally teaches truth about God.

• Do not forsake corporate worship because you don't like the music. Acknowledge your need to have regular fellowship with the church body.

Real Life Wisdom:

In this way, worship and spirituality are grounded in the work of Jesus Christ incarnate in this history, who died on the wood of the cross, left the tomb empty, and ascended to heaven. He gave the church the calling to proclaim, sing, and enact His mighty saving deeds and to live in union with Him and His purposes for this world while we anticipate the new heavens and the new earth.–Robert Webber

Savvy Resources for Additional Study:

Unceasing Worship: Biblical Perspectives on Worship and the Arts
By Harold Best (Downers Grove, IL: InterVarsity Press, 2003)
Author also of *Music Through the Eyes of Faith*

Sacred Actions of Christian Worship
By Robert Webber (Hendrickson Publishers, 1995)

www.ancientfutureworship.com

PROBLEMS IN CULTURE

> And do not be conformed to this world, but be transformed by the renewing of your mind, that you may prove what *is* that good and acceptable and perfect will of God.
> **Romans 12:2**

11.
WHERE DO I DRAW THE LINE ON ENTERTAINMENT OPTIONS?

Real Life Question:

Where do I draw the line on entertainment options for myself? Film, television, and art can all be used to share truth about our culture, but when does it cause me to sin?

Hollywood definitely has the attention of many young people in our culture, as well as older generations. Going to the movies is a favorite pastime of many Americans, but as Christians there are films and other forms of entertainment that can compete for our attention in negative ways. The savvy Christian knows when to say "no" to the latest blockbuster and when to say "yes."

Real Life Case Study:

The singles' group at First Baptist is gearing up for an all-night movie festival. Pastor Les is organizing the event and decides to call a meeting with some of the leaders of the group.

"Hey all, thanks for showing up. As I was planning for this event, I wanted it to be an outreach to those that don't come on Sundays. But I also wanted to borrow your consciences to help me in my selection process. I know what kind of movies I like, but I realized I don't know what kind of movies most of you like."

"I think it is great you are asking our opinion. I would be disappointed if we ended up with all Arnold Schwarzenneger movies," commented Kim.

"I just have one request," protested Sam. "No chick flicks. We need wide appeal here."

"Well, I really would like us to look past our own preferences and think about some of the moral dilemmas we might face with certain movies. I also think it is important that the movies promote meaningful discussion for us," shared Pastor Les. "So, I need to borrow your consciences collectively, so I can be sure our event doesn't offend anyone or cause someone to focus on the wrong things in our culture. So let's talk about some guidelines before we start picking our favorites …"

1. Think about the last movie you went to see with a friend or your family. Did you feel like you were informed enough to know whether or not it would compromise your values? Did you sense it was blatantly unchristian?

2. Take a moment and trace the themes of the movie. What positive message was there? Negative?

3. Read Proverbs 4:23; Philippians 4:8-9. What are some boundaries you have placed on movies to help you "guard your heart"? Other forms of entertainment?

4. Why do you think the entertainment industry has such great influence in our culture today?

5. What kind of music do you listen to? What attracts you to listen to a certain artist?

Real Life Lessons:

Sometimes it is hard to know how to spend our money and time on entertainment. The Christian should be careful not to view entertainment as a mindless act, but rather something that has the power to affect our hearts and minds at a very deep level. Our leisurely activities are not just acts of play to pass the time away. We are to bring ourselves to each moment of life if we believe all of life is sacred.

First, we should consider our own life experience and walk with God to help us determine what is appropriate to hear on the radio or see on a movie screen. For example, maybe in high school you were into heavy metal bands and were drunk and high every Friday night with your buddies. For you, rock music has a tendency to make you want to escape and drink again.

Or maybe you grew up in a strict, even legalistic, household that viewed the movie theater as the house of the devil. Maybe even playing cards was wrong, and you were taught that God could never show up in certain activities. Now you realize God can speak very redemptive things to your heart through film and playing cards can be a great vehicle in getting friends over for fellowship.

Building on life experience, you also need to know yourself well.

Much of the boundaries you determine will be based upon how honest you are with yourself. If you know you are a very visual person and really struggle with abstaining from sex with your girlfriend, then you should probably not see certain movies, or maybe you wait until they are released on DVD so you can fast-forward through a sensual scene instead of just sitting there, vulnerably watching it.

When we read Scripture, it seems clear that everyone is tempted in some way. And temptation itself is not an act of sin. Temptation can happen at work or on our own leisure time. We know Jesus was tempted in every way that we are, yet He remained without sin. Our desires should not be self-centered, lacking in self-control, or destructive (see Deuteronomy 5:21, Exodus 15:9) no matter what we are doing. Yet within God's economy and His rule, there is great freedom (2 Corinthians 3:17) where a Christian can live and thrive.

Good entertainment choices naturally flow out of grateful Christians. Sometimes entertainment has no other objective other than to overstimulate our senses, falsely persuading us that the world has enticing options that are much more exhilarating than can be found in the Christian life. There is an arrogance in such self-indulgence. But if we are truly seeking God's desires, we can resist such a lie that tells us we need more—whether it is more sex, more money, more power. Living out our lives with gratitude toward God safeguards our hearts from wanting to be swayed by what the world says is the good life.

Finally, a humble posture also can help us make right choices. Simply by remaining humble before God, we are acknowledging that we need His help and counsel. Often that is found outside our own conventional wisdom. Humility also allows us to put others first. What is a temptation to one is not to another. Paul says, "take care that this liberty of yours does not somehow become a stumbling block to the weak" (1 Corinthians 8:9). A humble friend will forego seeing a film or going to a concert when he knows their friend may struggle with a certain sin. Don't engage in entertainment just because you can. Other lives are also influenced by your choices.

Be wise and always take your Christian worldview with you when you are watching TV, going to a concert, or headed to the movies.

Real Life Strategies:

● Read Christian movie reviews and do research before you actually buy your tickets.

● Be creative in your own leisure time. Find new ways you can support the arts in your community. Visit your art museum or join a book review club.

● Don't view entertainment as a mindless exercise. Realize its powerful ability to portray truth and beauty.

Real Life Wisdom:

Leisure is not a state of being free from demands, not a noun, not an adjective describing time, not play. Leisure is work a commitment to activity whereby fine character is built.—Aristotle

Savvy Resources for Additional Study:

For recommended movies and reviews, visit Chuck Colson's BreakPoint ministry (www.breakpoint.org) and Focus on the Family (www.fotf.org).

Walking on Water: Reflections on Faith and Art
By Madeleine L'Engle (Wheaton, Ill: Harold Shaw Publishers, 1980.)

Hollywood Worldviews
By Brian Godawa

The Liberated Imagination: Thinking Christianly about the Arts
By Leland Ryken (Wheaton, Ill: Harold Shaw Publishers, 1989)

**But seek first
the kingdom
of God and His
righteousness,
and all these
things shall be
added to you.**

Matthew 6:33

12.
HOW DO
I FIGHT
CONSUMERISM?

Real Life Question:

How do I fight consumerism in an age when more is always better? Can I love Jesus and things?

There are more spending choices today than ever. Temptation to buy and acquire hit us over and over throughout our day. We find ourselves dreaming, if I just had this newer version of . . .

Real Life Case Study:

Jill rose to the top of her company fast. She found herself exhilarated by the title, the paycheck, and the social status. She felt like this was the big dream she always had hoped for. Yet at the end of the day, there was a gnawing feeling in the pit of her stomach that she just kept ignoring. She knew she was neglecting her family.

Jill and Jason had two kids and both put in about fifty hours at the office. Jason tried to travel when Jill wasn't. Schedules were complex, and the kids seemed to be more and more unhappy at each passing day.

"Marlee, what is wrong with you? I just bought you that new Barbie Jeep you wanted and you act up like this? You don't know how hard Mommy and Daddy work for our family."

"Mommy, I don't care about that Jeep anymore. I'm just lonely. You never have time for me."

Jill's stomach grew tight and tears flowed down her cheeks. What had she done? Did she buy into the great lie that money makes everyone happy?

"Sweetheart, Mommy knows she hasn't had time for you. I promise, it's going to change. I'll see if my boss will take me off the travel team for a few months."

Today, it is easy to buy into the mindset that looking good and having everything leads to a fulfilling life. Unfortunately the church has not escaped this mentality. Think for a moment about the families you know in your own church. Do you feel consumerism has got a hold of Christians, just as much as the world?

Christians know that a fulfilling life is not found in material things, but our culture bombards us continually with another message. We live in a time when shopping is now a pastime, prom night costs around five hundred dollars, kids drive brand new SUVs as their first car, and parents cannot seem to keep up with the demand, no matter how many promotions come their way. Yet even though children have more materially than past generations, they seem to battle depression more than ever. Why are we buying into the belief system of consumerism?

1. Do you feel like you have bought into the lie that *more* is always better? Why or why not? How do you protect yourself from falling into consumerism as a way of life?

2. Do you personally think that consumerism is affecting Christians just as much as nonbelievers? What do your conversations center around when you are with your Christian friends?

3. Write down what you believe is the meaning of life. How does this clash with the belief system of consumerism?

4. Read the story of the Rich Young Ruler found in Luke 18:18-23. Write out your reflections about this story and what stands out to you in the passage. Why do you think Jesus asked him for all his possessions and not just some?

Real Life Lessons:

According to a George Barna study, over half of evangelicals believe the following statement: "The purpose of life is enjoyment and personal fulfillment."[1] The sentiment seems to have found its way into the mind of many Christians and has colored how we live out our faith.

But this should not be true of those that have committed their life to Christ. A Christian worldview does not point to material wealth as the road to a fulfilling life, nor does it place personal fulfillment as the chief end goal. Somewhere along the way, we have come to see money as the key to success and happiness. Consumerism really is a new belief system that is clashing with our Christian worldview, and we find ourselves trying to serve both belief systems.

Though not popular to say, we were never meant to live our lives with the end goal being happiness. The Christian should be aiming for something much higher, something found outside of the self, toward the needs of others. But unfortunately many Christians aren't convinced that money can't buy happiness.

Sometimes it is easy to think, *if I could just win the lottery my problems would be over.* Take some time to read about some of the instant lottery winners. Journalists have reported story after story of the ill turn life takes for some. Some have lost their money to poor investments, scam artists, have become recluses, or have ended up alcoholics in complete despair. Money did not prove to be an answer for many.

Christians need to know that there is nothing wrong with working hard and improving the life of your family. Naturally we desire to give our kids what we didn't have. But wealth should never consume our life goals. First Timothy 6:10 says the love of money is evil, not money itself. The savvy Christian lives for God's purposes, understanding how possessions and wealth can be used in redemptive ways, and lives a life investing in others, not just in the stock market.

Self-indulgence is the foundation of consumerism. Very easily we justify something we can't afford because life is short and hard and we need to have some fun. The fact is the more we possess, the worse off we can be when it comes to pursuing a meaningful life. Possessions have a tendency to possess us, if we let them.

That is why God shows us that He is a jealous God. Anything that competes with our relationship with Him can harm us. We can choose things very easily as our false god or idol. The first commandment says, "you shall have no other gods before me." His jealousy isn't a selfish, self-serving kind of jealousy. Our God knows what we need and what is best for our relationship with

Him. He cares about our well-being. Real happiness is found living for God's higher purposes—in right relationship with Him and others. We have to be brave and challenge society's myths, such as consumerism, that try to shape and even destroy the life God intended for us to have.

Real Life Strategies:

- Think about what you really treasure and see if you feel materialism is negatively affecting your relationship with God.

- Protect your relationship with God above all things. Make sure you are investing your life in the kingdom's work, not just the material world.

- Find time to be grateful for all God has given you. Gratitude is a great cure in overcoming selfishness.

- Make sure you examine your motives as you pursue career, work, and financial reward.

- Put relationships above possessions.

Real Life Wisdom:

The truth is that happiness demands far more and far less than the sum total of our possessions and pleasures. What we truly long for isn't boundless riches. What we desire is a sense of significance and value—of human dignity. –Chuck Colson

Savvy Resources for Additional Study:
Search the Web and read about lottery winners who found money was not the answer to their problems

The Good Life: Seeking Purpose, Meaning, and Truth in your Life
By Chuck Colson (Tyndale, 2005)

Read about L. Dennis Kozlowski, quoted in "The Most Aggressive CEO," Business Week Online, May 28, 2001, http://www.businessweek.com/magazine/content/01_22/b3734001.htm

13.

CAN THE RICH INHERIT THE KINGDOM OF GOD?

> Then Jesus said to His disciples, "Assuredly, I say to you that it is hard for a rich man to enter the kingdom of heaven. And again I say to you, it is easier for a camel to go through the eye of a needle than for a rich man to enter the kingdom of God."
>
> **Matthew 19:23-24**

Real Life Question:

Can the rich inherit the kingdom of God? Can we really be saved, just continuing in our lifestyles being the wealthiest country?

Most of us have more material wealth than our parents and generations past. We also expect to give our children more than what we had. More never seems to be quite enough. If we just had a millions dollars, all would be right with the world, or would it?

Real Life Case Study:

It was one extravagant fortieth birthday bash for Karen Kozlowski, later to be watched by the Supreme Court in Manhattan. The famous L. Dennis Kozlowski held his party honoring his wife on the island of Sardinia off the coast of Italy, which was roughly $28,000 per guest. A homemade video was used as evidence to convict Kozlowski of one of the biggest corporate scandals of our day—grand larceny, stealing some $600,000 from his company, Tyco.

Kozlowski knew how to throw a party. Jimmy Buffet performed for $250,000. Women jumping out of cakes, an ice-sculpture fountain, and a replica of Michelangelo's *David* urinating vodka, set the mood. The most lavish production was the poolside ballet, where dancers celebrated youth, beauty, and eroticism. His life had grown accustomed to excess.

When the headlines reported the Tyco scandal in 2003, no one could believe that someone could get away with such a huge crime. Sadly, it was Dennis' quick rise to the top that was his slow death. His party was a statement about his lifestyle and his love for money.

Growing up in a poor section of Newark, his parents couldn't even afford to own a home. He put himself through college and met business tycoon Joseph Gaziano, the chairman and CEO of Tyco Laboratories. He hired Dennis, and that is when his pocketbook grew, but his life turned into one tragedy after another.

Quickly, he moved into a $900,000 home with his wife, Angie. As soon as he rose to the top, his marriage suffered and they divorced. He was known for his successful mergers and acquisitions which kept his board happy. His was known for making up his own rules in business as well in his extra marital affairs. At an all time high, he reached a salary of $170 million in 1999, landing him among the highest paid CEOs.

Quickly Dennis had made a lifestyle change from family man to business tycoon, and finally criminal. Money and power were a toxic mix for Dennis.

1. Have you known someone who has gone from rags to riches? Did you see their priorities change?

2. How can money change our thinking?

3. Do you know someone who has been able to keep God first, but it still very wealthy?

4. Read Luke 15:11-31. How did the son's inheritance affect his soul? When did he realize that he desired more from life?

Real Life Lessons:

Jesus talks about money more than any other topic during His earthly ministry. He knew of its allure and how it can tempt the human heart. For some reason, more is never quite enough for most of us. There is always one more thing we want to buy.

Most Americans would say that they are not rich, yet in comparison to the rest of the world, we are blessed in every way. Things monetarily come easier in this generation and it is difficult to teach children the value of a dollar. We forget how fortunate we are, thinking we always need to acquire more.

We definitely need to take heed and listen to Jesus' warning about money. In Matthew 19:23-26, He tells the disciples how difficult it is for a rich man to enter the kingdom of God. A camel, the largest animal in the region, and an eye of a needle, the smallest object, were contrasted to show how difficult it can be for a wealthy man to be saved. But Jesus also explains that all things are possible with God. The rich can tend to rely on the security money affords them, and not on God as their source. Most of us would openly admit that we pray more when we are struggling. When we have a need, we are more inclined to spend time with our Heavenly Father.

But money in and of itself is not evil. The Apostle Paul tells us that it is the love of money that is wrong. To be rich can be a distraction in our lives. Our wealth can be hard to share if we are too attached to it. The wealthy can inherit the kingdom of God if their life is submitted to God. Without the saving work of Jesus, none of us can be saved, rich or poor. But there seems to be more of an obvious need for God's help when we are lacking something. Mother Teresa once said that America was the wealthiest nation, but the poorest spiritually. When we have lack, there is more room for God to move and less tendency for us to rely on our own strength. We are more inclined to lean on Him.

The church has reaped many blessings, and our wealth can work against us. Various celebrities have spoken out against the Christian community that seems to be complacent about the poor and the sick around the world. Our critics can be God's gift to us to help us see where we have fallen short of our biblical mandate. We should be asking ourselves, am I doing all I can to reach out the poor? How can I help with the AIDS crises in Africa? What is my biblical mandate toward the weak and the helpless? Have my own monetary blessings caused me to ignore those that are in need?

But the verdict is that the rich and poor both can be saved. God has come to save all of us, no matter what our economic status may be. But don't be surprised if He asks us to give up an idol, whether it is money or status, so that He can get His foot in the door.

Real Life Strategies:

• No matter what your economic status is, realize we are stewards of His resources, and that all that we have is really His.

• Money can cause us to neglect our spiritual lives.

• Money can be used to further the kingdom of God when we allow God to be God of our finances.

Real Life Wisdom:

We have been taught false principles by the world in which we live. The plumb line for truth is God's Word, not a college textbook or a standard practice. God's Word teaches a set of principles most of us haven't heard in the media or in the classroom. Our greatest wealth from God is our salvation. It never ends.
–Larry Burkett

Savvy Resources for Additional Study:
Take time and read the various references to money in both the Old and New Testament. List common themes that you find about wealth.

http://en.wikipedia.org/wiki/Dennis_Kozlowski

He has shown
you, O man,
what is good;
and what does
the **LORD**
require of you
but to do justly,
to love mercy,
and to walk
humbly with
your God?
Micah 6:8

14.

HOW DO I SAY "NO" TO ONE MORE THING?

Real Life Question:

My days are maxed out and it seems I'm always trying to catch up. I want to make time for things that matter, but it seems the daily duties just eat up all the time I have. What can I do to slow down?

Though we have many modern conveniences that allow us to be more efficient, it seems productivity just adds more pressures and demands. We feel like we are being steamrolled by progress, often on the edge of complete burnout. To wake up and face another day, feels like just one more mountain to climb against the clock.

Real Life Case Study:

Jack was a successful doctor with a godly wife and great kids. He made a lot of money, but it didn't ever seem to be enough for the growing needs of their family. Soccer. Uniforms. School tuition. Game boys. Cell phones. Computers. College tuition.

Jack and Jane had been members of their church for the past fifteen years and felt like their boys really had received solid teaching and would be grounded when they were ready for college. Jack knew the church had given them a strong spiritual heritage, but it seems he never had time to give back to those that had given so much to him and his family.

Working eighty hours a week was average for Jack since medical school. There just wasn't time for much else. His friend Darrell had been going to a prayer breakfast each week and invited Jack to attend. Reluctant to commit, Jack decided to attend and figured he had to eat breakfast anyway.

To Jack's surprise, he found he had more energy after spending time with friends he knew from church. He received prayer support before going in to see his patients, and he realized he has missed out on relationships for many years. He was asked by another doctor there if he might donate some of his time to the children's home for a Christmas event. Jack always wanted to donate his medical services to charity, but never made time for it. He quickly said, "Yes, I'd love to help." He knew God was asking him to help, and knew it would require sacrifice and changing his priorities.

On his drive to the office, he began to think of Jane and the boys. He had been a good provider but not a father or husband that was involved relationally. He began to pray and cry out to God for wisdom on what he could do to take time and invest more in his family, church, and friends. Before he left his car, he promised God he would work less and give more to Him in serving others.

1. In what ways can you identify with Jack and Jane?

2. How well do you think you manage your time and your household?

3. Read Luke 10:38-42. Hospitality is a very important gift to others and Jesus did not disregard Martha's service. Relationally, how was Martha depriving herself?

4. Do you feel like you spend more time with daily tasks or with people? Would you classify yourself as someone caught up in the rat race?

Real Life Lessons:

If asked, most of us would plead guilty of living an overloaded life. Our lives are overloaded with technology, work, debt, pollution, ministry activities, noise, stressful decisions, and pressure. Taking time to share a cup of coffee with a friend seems like a luxury.

With all the demands of life looming over us, sometimes it is hard to see a solution. Dr. Richard Swenson, author of the book *Margin*, points out the need for Christians to recognize that we are often overextended and cannot actually live out our faith effectively because of the demands we have placed on ourselves.

For the Christian, our love for God and others should never be jeopardized by the busyness of life. Micah 6:8 tells us what is required of us: to do justly, love mercy, and walk humbly with God. If our lives don't allow time for these biblical expressions of our faith, we are missing out on God's best for us.

When we get too busy to worship God, serve our church, or meet a need of a stranger, we have lost margin. If every moment of the day is full the rim with tasks, we will continue to feel burnout and stress. God created us as spiritual beings and when we neglect our relationship with God, we find other distractions to fill that hole.

Think for a moment what your week looks like. How many things have eternal value? How many things nourish your relationship with God and your family? Do you often pass by someone on the side of the road that could use your help, but you are late to an appointment and too busy to stop? Most likely, there is a greater need to find margin your life.

Yes, we all have responsibilities and daily obligations that require time, but they should never control us. As we see in Jesus' ministry, people always came first. Jesus, no doubt, could claim He was a busy man. But He never was too busy for those that presented a need to Him. He always took time to show do justly, to love mercy, and do His Father's will. When we have lost this rhythm of life, we have lost what matters in God's economy.

To have margin in our lives takes planning and a desire to resist the cultural tide pulling us toward more progress. Better homes, better jobs, and better bank accounts aren't always what God desires for us. The problem that progress has brought to our lives affects the core of what we really were created to do: worship God and love others. Yes, we have nicer cars and houses, but relationally we have not invested what God would desire of us.

With God's help, we can live a healthy life with thriving marriages and relationships if we put relationships in their rightful place. When we do that, we will have time to help our neighbor when they need a hand. Or we will be able to make a meal for someone recovering from illness and have the time needed. We won't have to abandon our communities to live in balance, but rather we will have the ability to serve.

Real Life Strategies:

- Pray about some activities you can give up to have more margin in your week.

- Make time to be together as a family that requires interaction and discussion.

- Identify the things that are keeping you from living a relationally healthy life.

- Realize sleep and rest are God's ideas.

Real Life Wisdom:

Today I imagined my inner self as a place crowded with pins and needles. How could I receive anyone in my prayer when there is no real place for them to be free and relaxed? When I am still so full of preoccupations, jealousies, angry feelings, anyone who enters will get hurt. I had a very vivid realization that I must create some free space in my innermost self so that I may indeed invite others to enter and be healed.—Henri Nouwen

Savvy Resources for Additional Study:
Margin: Restoring Emotional, Physical, Financial, and Time Reserves to Overloaded Lives
By Richard Swenson (2004)

Genesee Diary
By Henri Nouwen

You are the light of the world. A city that is set on a hill cannot be hidden. Nor do they light a lamp and put it under a basket, but on a lampstand, and it gives light to all *who are* in the house. Let your light so shine before men, that they may see your good works and glorify your Father in heaven.

Matthew 5:14-16

15.
CAN MY CHRISTIAN WORLDVIEW REALLY MAKE A DIFFERENCE?

Real Life Question:

How can my Christian worldview make a difference in society when there are so many other stronger voices of influence? Are the other opposing voices stronger or just more pervasive?

It is easy to take a look at our culture and feel defeated in turning the cultural tide toward a just, moral place to raise our families. Most Christians don't have a public platform to carry their convictions and beliefs. Yet we know we have a biblical mandate to be salt and light in our world. When our culture is opposed to God's laws, as Christians we know there are consequences and society will suffer. How do we make a difference?

Real Life Case Study:

One of the greatest moral achievements in society happened in the British Empire during the end of the eighteenth century. William Wilberforce recognized the grave sin of his country—the slave trade, the empire's livelihood.

As a politician he faced immense odds and was criticized and despised. Slavery was a morally accepted practice and vital to the economy. His opponents were politicians, powerful businessmen, national heroes, and the royal family. Wilberforce made many enemies during his time in parliament, but he showed remarkable perseverance. For nearly fifty years, he fought to overturn slavery. He was willing to be called a fool for the sake of Christ.

William Wilberforce understood that his faith had to matter to more than just himself. At age twenty-five, he became a Christian and wanted to go into ministry full-time. But through prayer and counsel, he realized God's plan was for him to pursue a career in politics and to champion the freedom of the oppressed. In his journal he wrote, "My walk, is a public one." Wilberforce knew that he had to try and make a difference, and God would guide him through the battles he would face.

1. Do you struggle with ways to influence the community around you? What are some wrongs you see in your community that you would like to see change?

2. What can we learn from the example of William Wilberforce and making our faith a public matter?

3. Do you feel like you have bought into the cultural lie that one life cannot make a difference? Reflect on some of the fears you might have of speaking boldly about your faith.

4. Read Matthew 5:13-16. Think about some ways that you are a light to your neighbor next door. Then think about some ways you that would enable you to be a louder voice among your non-Christian friends.

Real Life Lessons:

Usually the only time we find Christians or churches featured in the news is when scandal is involved. Rarely do we hear the secular airwaves promote the positive influence Christians have on society. This anti-Christian sentiment that we often feel has caused many to retreat and not believe that one voice could ever make a difference. But as Christians, we know in God's economy one life can make all the difference in the world.

Though the world is often quick to make Christianity out to be foolish, God's truth has proven to actually work in the laws of society. When we come to Christ, we find personal restoration, but this transformation should also spill out into our own life setting. God's truth has the power to create civilized societies, preserve freedom, and soften the hearts of the hardest criminal. That is why we have to share the hope we have been given. Our faith was not meant to be some kind of private blessing, but it is to overflow to others giving society a hope and a future as well. We are co-laborers with Christ in transforming all aspects of culture—the arts, education, the media, politics, and science. All of life is sacred, and God wants us to be available to speak of His truth.

Take for example the life of William Wilberforce. He understood his value and his identity are rooted in Christ. There is a vast difference in the Christian worldview about the worth of one life and that of the postmodern view. The Christian view sees the intrinsic value of worth in all of life. Nothing is too small or insignificant in God's eyes. But for the average modern thinker, only the famous, rich, or person of status has hope of marking the world. Wilberforce understood his potential to fight cultural evils, even as just one man living out his conviction that slavery was an evil of his day that had to be confronted no matter how many times his efforts failed.

Christians especially need to realize the power of Christ at work in them and not succumb to believing their life has no divine purpose. If we believe we can make no difference, we can find ourselves easily in a slothful position. Dorothy Sayers warned against complacency and sloth and said, "the sin which believes in nothing, cares for nothing, seeks to know nothing, interferes with nothing, enjoys nothing, loves nothing, hates nothing, find purpose in nothing, lives for nothing, and only remains alive because there is nothing it would die for."

So yes, absolutely the Christian voice matters, no matter how small or seemingly insignificant. Christians need to pray for courage and step out into the public square to be heard and see what God does with the efforts.

Real Life Strategies:
- Never underestimate God's plan for your life and how He can use you right where you are today.

- Check to make sure you have not bought into the cultural lie that one voice cannot make a difference.

- Pray about how you might live out the convictions God has placed on your heart.

• Think about someone you know whose courage and persistence made a difference in their community. Thank God for their example and heroes of our faith that do spur us on to do good works.

Real Life Wisdom:

You have never talked to a mere mortal. Nations, cultures, arts, civilization—these are mortal, and their life is to ours as the life of gnat. But it is immortals whom we joke with, work with, marry, snub, and exploit—immortal horrors or everlasting splendors. –William Wilberforce

Savvy Resources for Additional Study:
Learn more about the remarkable life of William Wilberforce at www.wilberforcecentral.org.

Doing Well and Doing Good: The Challenge to the Christian Capitalist
By Richard John Neuhaus (New York: Doubleday, 1992).

Redeeming the Time: A Christian Approach to Work and Leisure
By Leland Ryken (Grand Rapids, MI: Baker Books, 1995).

Then Paul, as his custom was, went in to them, and for three **Sabbaths** reasoned with them from the **Scriptures**, explaining and demonstrating that the **Christ** had to suffer and rise again from the dead, and *saying,* "This **Jesus** whom I preach to you is the **Christ**." And some of them were persuaded; and a great multitude of the devout Greeks, and not a few of the leading women, joined Paul and Silas.

Acts 17:2-4

16.
HOW CAN I TALK OPENLY WITH OTHERS ABOUT CHRISTIANITY?

Real Life Question:

Is it okay to dialogue with people of another faith? Will it tempt me to think Christianity really isn't the only true faith?

Sometimes we have not fully allowed ourselves to be confronted with another worldview, and it can be intimidating and can even shake our faith. There are so many different belief systems out there that are all bidding for our attention and claim to be valid.

Real Life Case Study:

Kelly's missions class required each person to experience worship in the context of another faith besides Christianity. She had never known a Muslim and wanted to know more of what they believed.

She arrived a bit scared but excited. Many women greeted her at the door and helped her find her place. Immediately, the women were asked to move to the back room, where they would worship. Only the men were permitted to go into the main sanctuary. Women and children watched through the screen door. Kelly felt exposed as the Muslim women all had their hair covered and were staring at her long blonde hair.

Kelly sat and prayed for the women in the room and observed their reverent posture with awe. They chanted and cried out to their god, as the Muslim minister read from the Koran. Kelly was struck by their discipline and obedience, but felt the cold walls of legalism around her.

After the service, one of the women came up to Kelly. She was not of Persian descent, and Kelly could tell she was American under the veil. "Hello, I am Kathy. I just converted to the Muslim faith and just wondered if you had any questions?"

"Hi, I'm Kelly. Well, I'm here for a class I'm taking and wanted to experience another form of worship. What was your faith before your conversion?"

"I was a Christian, but then I met my husband, who shared his Muslim faith. What I really could never understand about Christianity was the doctrine of the Trinity. Islam is truly a monotheistic faith, and I believe now I am worshiping the one true God."

"Oh, I see. I've learned a lot just from observing."

"I also find that there is a greater devotion to God in the Muslim faith and I've learned a lot about discipline and prayer", shared Kathy.

"Yes, I have to say I feel convicted about my own prayer life after seeing the fervency in which women pray here at the mosque.... It was really nice to meet you. God bless you."

"Nice to meet you. Please come back anytime."

Kelly left feeling a little uncomfortable, a little wiser, and a little more thankful.

1. Have you ever participated in a worship service that was not at a Christian church? If so, recall your experience and what you learned.

2. How can other faiths serve to sharpen our own faith?

3. Read Colossians 4:5-6. Think about some opportunities that you might have around you that you've missed. When sharing your faith with others, have you found it hard to not get defensive?

4. Think for a moment about another faith besides Christianity that you know a little about. What is enticing about it? Do you think there are similarities that it shares with Christianity? Take a moment to compare and contrast.

Real Life Lessons:

Have you ever found your faith challenged by someone else? Dialoguing with others of another faith can be intimidating, but something very healthy for our faith. We shouldn't just hang out with Christians or talk with Christians about our faith. We need to talk with those that would disagree with us. It can take some effort and intentional planning to be around those with whom you can bring up faith and religion in a comfortable setting.

Take for example, Kelly. She left her cross-cultural experience feeling convicted about exercising more discipline in her prayer life when she witnessed firsthand the discipline of the Muslim women. Sometimes we can learn truthful things about ourselves when we take time to look at the spiritual life of someone else.

You may find it uncomfortable to disagree with someone, especially if it is a friend and not just a casual acquaintance. But we can learn to disagree respectfully in efforts to know what we believe with greater clarity and conviction. If our viewpoint is never challenged, what do we learn? And we really can't know firsthand what another faith believes without talking with someone who has lived out that worldview. We have to engage each other in conversation.

When talking with someone from a different faith, you may be surprised to find that they would agree with many Christian principles. That is because all of God's truth is around us. He is not just confined to the walls of Christianity. Universal truths are really God's transcendent truths that rise above culture, time, and religion. His truth holds all things together and humanity cannot escape it, even outside of the Christian tradition.

Mutual respect is important when talking with another. Sometimes it is easy to come across as being superior to another, and you may want to say, "How could you even believe that? It makes no sense at all ... don't you see?" Humility is very important part of sharing your faith. Every person is worthy of respect.

If you find yourself in a debate, think of it as a positive opportunity to share your faith. When we are pressed to give the best possible answer, our thinking is sharpened and it encourages us to really think about what we believe. We begin to evangelize without even realizing it. Oftentimes we rely on the words we have heard in our Sunday school classes or church services, not really making our faith our own. Dialoguing can make our faith real to others and to ourselves.

Remember the great theologian C.S. Lewis. Lewis was a professed atheist, but soon found himself heavily influenced by the worldview of Christians, one being author J.R.R. Tolkien. As colleagues and friends, Lewis and Tolkien spent much of their time together debating, yet allowing one another the freedom to disagree. Slowly, Lewis began to find himself believing in theism. He wrote during is pre-conversion period, "I felt as if I were a man of snow at long last beginning to melt." Later he came to conclude that Christ was the way. Lewis' sharp thinking continues to influence Christianity today, laypersons, academicians, and the Church at large.

Real Life Strategies:
- Don't pretend to have all the answers. No one does.

- Make efforts to find truth in someone else's religious beliefs. This doesn't mean you endorse or adhere to another faith. Rather it can provide common ground and a means to discuss truth at greater length.

- Seek out opportunities that would place you among non-Christians.

Real Life Wisdom:
Evangelism is not an option for the Christian life.–Luis Palau

In faith there is enough light for those who want to believe and enough shadows to blind those who don't. – Blaise Pascal

Savvy Resources for Additional Study:
Mere Christianity
By C.S. Lewis (New York: Touchstone, 1996)

Scaling the Secular City
By J.P. Moreland (Grand Rapids: Baker, 1987)

Handbook of Christian Apologetics
By Peter Kreeft (Downers Grove, Ill.: InterVarsity Press, 1994).

Before I formed you in the womb I knew you; before you were born I sanctified you; I ordained you a prophet to the nations.
Jeremiah 1:5

17.
WHAT SHOULD I KNOW ABOUT THE STEM CELL DEBATE?

Real Life Question:

What should I know about stem cell research? I'm not up on the latest breakthroughs in medical research, but probably need to be more aware of what is going on ethically. Should Christians support it?

Technology is changing so quickly, and I don't know how to keep up with the all the ethical dilemmas we are facing in the twenty-first century.

Real Life Case Study:

A few months into Amy's pregnancy, she noticed things weren't quite right. Worry and sleepless nights followed weeks of prenatal testing. Amy finally received the terrible news that her baby had a genetic disorder.

"We can terminate the pregnancy, Amy. It is up to you and your husband."

"No, that is not an option for us," pleaded Amy.

"To avoid this happening in the future, you may wish to consider using a fertility clinic and donating your eggs to science, so that embryonic stem cell research can help future children."

"Well, thanks for the information, Doctor, but my husband and I will love this child no matter how long we are blessed with this life."

"Well, you might want to think about how you vote in this next election. It may help you grow a healthy family in the future. Sometimes people confuse an embryo with a fetus. They don't realize an embryo is no bigger than a dot."

Amy collected her thoughts and interjected, "Since when does size determine a person's value? All are significant in God's sight."

"Amy, I'm your doctor and I just feel it is important to inform you of all your medical options."

"I understand. Just don't expect me to change my beliefs to further medical research. I know God has a plan and purpose for my baby, even if we will only have this child for a very short time. Without question, we are proceeding with the pregnancy."

1. What would you do if you were facing the reality of having an unhealthy child who might even suffer? What would you be tempted to do?

2. How does the doctor's worldview clash with a Christian worldview?

3. Those that are not opposed to embryonic stem cell research tend to favor a utilitarian ethic, which is a belief that would say it is always best to work toward the greater

good of all people, even at the expense of an individual. Read Matthew 5:21-42. How did Jesus show his concern for the crowds and the individual?

4. A utilitarian belief system would also pursue pleasure and happiness as the end goal of life. How does Jesus' ethic differ from a utilitarian ethic?

5. How do you think stem cell research might affect your family and their future choices?

Real Life Lessons:

Stem cells are the master cells of the human body and can potentially develop into every type of cell. This is why medical research is exploring the benefits of both embryonic and adult stem cells to cure diseases such as diabetes, Parkinson's disease, cancer, heart conditions, and many other serious ailments.

We often hear more about the stem cell research debate surrounding political campaigns than other times, but this debate is often a headline in the daily news. Celebrities have taken strong stands in favor of stem cell research. But when discussing this hot topic in the media, it isn't always clear what type of stem cell research is being addressed. Ethically, there is a vast difference in embryonic stem cell research and adult stem cell research.

The late Christopher Reeve aggressively promoted research using human embryos from donor and fertility clinics. For this type of stem cell research, human embryos are sacrificed in hopes of finding a cure for diseases. But we have to be careful not to be misguided when we hear the word "cure." The end should never justify the means. Science clearly says that life begins at conception. So for science, as well as the Christian, a fertilized egg is a human life. Ethically, embryonic stem cell research causes many dilemmas for a Christian, as it involves the death of human life. In addition, research has failed to prove the embryonic stem cells are any more effective than when using adult stem cells.

Adult stem cells, however, do not destroy a human life. These cells come from the developed human body, such as from the umbilical cord blood. Adult stem cell research is proving to be effective and strides are being made toward finding cures, but not at the expense of Christian ethics. Christians can support this type of research without there being any need to sacrifice a life. Joni Eareckson Tada, a quadriplegic for over thirty-five years, promotes this type of research and is very outspoken about the benefits of pursuing adult stem cell research. Being a wheelchair for most of her life, she has chosen not to compromise the sanctity of life for her own happiness and well being. Tada says, "My husband and I support spinal-cord-injury research, but not to the degree that the benefits of any potential cure outweigh serious moral questions, effects on society, and whether it is an affront to God."

Christians need to be equipped to give an answer for issues that deal with the making and taking of life. We are familiar with the various issues surrounding abortion, but might not understand where biotechnology is headed in the way of stem cell research. There is a great need to make efforts to be informed and understand the consequences of stem cell research. We need to realize that sometimes general principles are easier to stand by than when we are talking about a loved one in our own life. Morally we need to be prepared and know what we believe about life, which includes the unborn.

Real Life Strategies:

● Take time to read about the debates regarding stem cell research. Don't view this topic as something that does not affect you and the future of your family.

● Read bioethicists that have a Christian worldview and are making efforts to preserve the sanctity of life.

● Don't think your vote doesn't count when election time comes around. Know what your local representatives believe about the stem cell research debate.

Real Life Wisdom:

The lives of all of us are jeopardized when life can be bought and sold, copied and replicated, altered and aborted and euthanized . . . We are vulnerable in a society that thinks nothing of creating a class of human beings for the purpose of lethal experimentation and exploitation.—Joni Eareckson Tada

Savvy Resources for Additional Study:
Playing God? Facing Everyday Ethical Dilemmas of Biotechnology
Hosted by Charles Colson, written by Tracey D. Lawrence
(Group Publishing: Loveland, 2004)

Stem Cells and Cloning
By David Prentice (Redwood, CA: Benjamin Cummings, 2002)

www.joniandfriends.org

Visit www.breakpoint.org for other resources for Christians that can help inform you about trends in bioethics.

And whenever
the time came
for Elkanah to
make an offering,
he would give
portions to
Peninnah his wife
and to all her sons
and daughters.
But to Hannah
he would give a
double portion,
for he loved
Hannah, although
the LORD had
closed her womb.
I Samuel 1:4-5

18.
WHAT SHOULD I KNOW ABOUT BIOTECHNOLOGY AND INFERTILITY?

Real Life Question:

Dealing with infertility has been difficult. We know we have options that we can pursue, but aren't sure if all possibilities medically are for us or not. What should we consider as we try and grow our family?

Infertility is a real problem for over 10 million couples in America. As the number of families dealing with this problem increases, there is a need for the church to have some answers in how to deal with this sensitive topic.

Real Life Case Study:

Janna and John dreamed of having at least eight children when they were first married. Both agreed that they would start a family right away. After a year of marriage, Janna began wondering what might be wrong and sought the advice of her doctor. Her doctor said she was infertile, but assured her that technology was really opening avenues for couples that did not exist before.

Janna and John soon met with the specialist who would be walking them through *in vitro* fertilization. Janna knew the risks, but could not imagine life without their own children. They moved full speed ahead with their treatments and remained hopeful.

"Janna, we have ten strong fertilized eggs that we can use through the process," reported Dr. Harris. "Obviously we will not insert all the embryos. So what we will do is try and insert three. Chances are, you will lose at least two, and one will take. Then if you miscarry all of them, we still have some embryos in reserve."

"What? I guess I was so excited about everything, I didn't realize . . . I didn't know we had ten embryos, just waiting in limbo. I guess I thought we would just insert one at a time."

"No. That is way too expensive for you to do it that way, with not a very big success rate. Having more inserted will increase your chances of pregnancy."

"Oh, I guess I just didn't understand all of this. We can't afford having ten children, but I guess that is really the reality of what could happen."

Janna had three embryos inserted and to the doctor's surprise, they had triplets. Life was going well and Janna and John were busy with their active toddlers. Then Janna received the letter from the clinic.

"John, what are we to do? The clinic says that our frozen embryos will be discarded if we do not use them by the end of this year. We have seven left. Had I known all of this, I would not have proceeded down this road."

"Janna, I know how tired you are with keeping up with the triplets. How can we possibly raise seven more kids and stay sane? I just don't know what the solution is, yet I know we have a moral obligation to do what God would want."

1. How does technology change how we view sex, marriage, and procreation?

2. Do you know of someone struggling with infertility? What are some of the struggles that they experienced in pursuing options?

3. Think about what you know about *in vitro* fertilization. List some of the moral dilemmas that might come up for a Christian.

4. Read about three women in the Bible and they dealt with infertility:

Sarai – Genesis 16:1-15
Rachel – Genesis 30:1-24
Hannah – 1 Samuel 1:1-28

How did Hannah respond to her infertility? Do you think pursuing various fertility treatments can challenge the sovereignty of God? Why or why not?

Real Life Lessons:

Infertility can be a touchy subject for the church to handle, but Christians are in need of answers in how to deal with this reality. This can be a difficult struggle in a marriage and it is very important for couples to receive wise, Christian counsel in what their options really are.

Consumerism has even found its way in procreation. Blonde hair, blue eyes, a certain IQ can all be listed as requirements of the potential donor. Men and women can go to a clinic and order what type of egg or sperm they want if they are infertile or just desire to have a child outside of marriage. For the Christian this mentality can pose some ethical problems.

For example, say a married couple has chosen to use donated sperm and have the embryos frozen that are not used. Tragically, the marriage ends and there is still a moral responsibility to attend to the frozen embryos. The embryos belong to both parties involved, and there is a tendency to treat them like property or a commodity. The ethical issues can cause great stress for all involved.

Or, perhaps a couple is going to use their own sperm and eggs and pursue *in vitro* fertilization (IVF). This procedure is not without real complications and moral issues, even if you choose not to freeze embryos. Most often women must take drugs to enable them to *super ovulate* so that there are many eggs to choose from. The doctor chooses only the "strongest" and "best" embryos for implantation and then there will be spares for disposal. Though not intended, there could be spares that will need to be discarded or frozen for later use. But even if the couple decides to implant additional embryos later, often the embryos don't even survive the thawing process. The fate of these embryos lies in the hands of technology and the success of the *in vitro* process, rather than the natural environment of the womb. There are over 400,000 "extra" frozen embryos in facilities across America. Christians need to be asking, should embryos even be frozen? Is this an ethical way to treat a human life?

There are other real, fulfilling options for infertile couples. Adoption is an option that mirrors the Gospel story. As God adopted us into His family lineage, a couple can experience the blessing of choosing a child to be a part of their family. For a child to learn they were actually chosen by their mother and father is a blessing and a legacy. James 1:27 says, "Religion that God our Father accepts as pure and faultless is this: to look after orphans and widows in their distress and to keep oneself from being polluted by the world." We know that God is very concerned for the orphans. Whether a Christian couple decides to pursue adoption or not, it is clear we have a biblical mandate to care for those without family.

There are pros and cons when pursuing domestic or international adoption, so talking with other Christian couples who have adopted can serve as a great resource of what steps to take first. Be prayerful and seek out the support of your church and strong believers who may have wisdom to share from their own faith and life experience. And, if infertility has not directly affected your family, every Christian should know how to treat and even counsel those needing support through this difficult struggle. Knowing what we believe about family, procreation, and ethical dilemmas is a part of our moral obligation and a testimony of our faith to the watching world.

Real Life Strategies:

- Try and find a Christian doctor when pursuing fertility treatments.

- Encourage your church to address bioethics.

- Think about what guiding principles you can use to make ethical issues when deciding to pursue IVF, fertility treatments, and other medical procedures that deal with the making of life.

Real Life Wisdom:

I am strongly opposed to creating fertilized eggs from "'donors" outside the immediate family. In my opinion, to engage in such activity would be to "play God"—to create human life outside the bonds of marriage. I believe most conservative Christians would agree that this practice is morally indefensible from a moral perspective.—James Dobson

Savvy Resources for Additional Study:

Visit Focus on the Family's Web site to read more about infertility issues
www.fotf.org

BioEngagement: Making a Christian Difference through Bioethics Today
Edited by Nigel Cameron, Scott Daniels, and Barbara J. White (Grand Rapids, MI: Eerdmans, 2000)

Matters of Life and Death
By Francis Beckwith and Norman L. Geisler
(Grand Rapids, MI: Baker Books, 1991).

103

Then he said, "O LORD God of my master Abraham, please give me success this day, and show kindness to my master Abraham. Behold, here I stand by the well of water, and the daughters of the men of the city are coming out to draw water. Now let it be that the young woman to whom I say, 'Please let down your pitcher that I may drink,' and she says, 'Drink, and I will also give your camels a drink'—let her be the one You have appointed for Your servant Isaac.

Genesis 24:12-14

19.
SHOULD A CHRISTIAN TRY ONLINE DATING?

Real Life Question:

Is it okay for Christians to try dating online? I'm so busy and can't always be where all the singles are. Am I a loser because I just can't find anyone in the conventional fashion?

Throughout American history, there are more women in attendance on Sundays than men. Singles ministries definitely reflect this ratio as well. This can create for a difficult dynamic. Women can feel even more pressure relationally if there are ten bright, sweet, spiritually strong females to one godly man. Men can feel like it is a meat market and all the women are after them, discouraging them from being themselves. The reality is sometimes our local church is the hardest place to meet someone, and the Christian single population can feel like finding a Christian spouse is next to impossible.

Real Life Case Study:

Steve loved his church and grew up with most of the families there. Now, in his thirties, most of his friends were married. He enjoyed the hospitality of many and would eat Sunday dinner with the families of his close buddies. He found himself envying all they had relationally at times, but was so grateful they didn't mind having a single guy around.

"Tim, I think I'm ready for marriage, but just not finding a match at our church. I love being with your family and really hope to be a dad someday. I don't want to start church hopping to just find a wife, so I think I'm going to try online dating," confessed Steve.

"Mmm . . . Well, what about Patty?"

"She's just gone through a really rough divorce, and I just don't feel comfortable with that situation," said Steve.

"Oh . . . what's wrong with Sue?"

"I think she likes her hamsters better than me."

"Oh . . . what about . . . ? Never mind. Yeah, I think you should try online dating. Why not?"

Steve is like many who find themselves working and living in communities where it is difficult to find a Christian spouse. Most people advise singles to find someone at church, but the reality is many singles avoid singles groups because they can be full of overly eager men and women who are too focused on finding a mate.

1. What are some advantages of meeting a date in person as opposed to meeting online?

2. What are some advantages of meeting someone online vs. in person?

3. Why do you think it can be increasingly difficult to find a Christian that is compatible for you in today's world?

4. Read Genesis 24. How did Isaac go about pursuing a spouse? Do you feel like it is okay for you to actively pursue marriage?

Real Life Lessons:

Many singles are struggling to find the right partner, or at least Mr. or Mrs. Maybe. There are reportedly 89 million singles in America and the church is realizing that they have neglected this huge demographic from the pulpit. For some Christians, it is impossible to find a mate that might be compatible because of their church, their job, and where they live. So what can a Christian do to proactively seek out a relationship? Perhaps online dating might be an alternative. There are some precautions to consider, just as there are with the conventional mode of dating. God might be calling you to step out on a limb and take a risk and try what online dating has to offer. Before you consider this, you may want to think through some of the real positives and negatives to this type of forum.

Positive: Most e-dating sites require you to fill out a personal profile and take a personality test to determine compatibility with someone. E-connections can help you think through things that you don't want in a mate before you have to meet someone. This can save someone from a lot of discouraging first-date experiences. You can weed through a lot of profiles and have the option of not choosing to e-mail a potential match. For those who are busy, this could be a timesaver, as relationships do require a lot of time.

Negative: In the online environment, some personalities are great communicators and some are not. Not everyone enjoys writing; therefore, some may sound mechanical and unfeeling because they would rather talk than write. And, you also may find it difficult to discern what is really meant in an e-mail. You don't have body language and voice inflexion, so chances are you are going to have times when you misunderstand a message. Taking time to make sure you understand what is really being said is important in getting to know someone online.

Positive: In the online environment, singles are often afraid that someone is portraying to be someone they are not. This is a real concern, but this is still true of those you date face to face. In fact, it may even be easier to spot false information online. If he claims to be an architect, but keeps misspelling it, then chances are he might not be telling you the truth. Or if someone claims that she is very active in church, yet doesn't seem to know what her church believes, you might quickly begin to wonder if this person really is that serious about her spiritual life.

Negative: When you are filling out your profile and completing the required information, realize that this isn't putting in an order for a perfect mate. In our consumer world, it is easy to buy into this mindset, especially when we can buy pretty much anything now online. Just because a machine matches you with someone doesn't mean this person will not have obvious faults. Everyone has faults and that's something that we have to accept when approaching any dating relationship.

Positive: Though there are still more women to men, even in the online environment, Christian singles still have more opportunity to meet Christians they would not normally meet. You may make some really good friends and learn and grow spiritually from a much broader range of Christianity than you would otherwise. This could be a very healthy, stretching experience that could enhance your own walk with God.

Before you meet, you should make sure you have prayed about the relationship and that you believe their faith is compatible with yours. Standards in dating should not be any different online. Never settle just because you are lonely.

When someone wants to move to the next step and exchange phone numbers and other personal information, make sure you have developed trust and moved beyond superficial conversations. Remember, the technological world is a world prone to superficial, grass roots information. This environment is not meant to provide a culture that is necessary to have a growing relationship, but can be a vehicle where it begins. As an e-dater, you cannot experience how someone interacts with others at work or socially, or how another lives out their faith on a day to day basis. To know if you really are compatible, someone must experience the highs and lows of life with someone before making any steps toward commitment. Realize its limitations, and if you find yourself not moving toward meeting, this probably isn't the right person for you.

Real Life Strategies:
- Be yourself in the online environment just as someone would expect you to be in conventional dating.

- Consider if you are in the same state. If you would have a difficult time with a long distance relationship, you may want to limit your scope of potential matches.

- Sometimes it is easier to be honest in the online environment, as there is not as much accountability. Be wise about that and refrain from saying anything you would not want someone to know if you were to meet. Everyone deserves to be treated with kindness.

Real Life Wisdom:
A dating relationship is not a private affair—when you are dating, your friends ask you questions, and they won't let you hid behind vagueness and innuendo.—Lauren Wiinner

Savvy Resources for Additional Study:
Habits of the High-Tech Heart: Living Virtuously in the Information Age
By Quentin J. Schultze *(Baker Academic: Grand Rapids, 2002)*

You may want to visit Christian online dating sites for more information.
www.eHarmony.com
www.christiancafe.com

I do not pray for these alone, but also for those who will believe in Me through their word; that they all may be one, as You, Father, are in Me, and I in You; that they also may be one in Us, that the world may believe that You sent Me.

John 17:20-21

20.
HOW DO I PURSUE UNITY WHEN THE CHURCH IS SO FRAGMENTED?

Real Life Question:

How can even try to pursue biblical unity when the church is so fragmented? I'm not sure who is right or wrong, but I know my non-Christian friends always bring up how we don't get along.

Our worst witness to the watching world is our fragmented testimony as a body of believers. How do seek out a unity that is doctrinally sound and relationally edifying?

Real Life Case Study:

Amy had just taken a position at her church in children's ministry. She was thrilled to serve in this way and knew the children's area had been neglected for some time due to budget restraints.

Her first project was to get rid of excess things in storage. The church had a school and was always cramped for space. Amy found they had double of many different toys, which was taking up a lot of room that they needed. She was amazed to see how much inventory was duplicated in some way. After a few days of sorting, she had a whole room of quality supplies that could assist any growing church nearby. She went to the church administration to see how they could steward the supplies best.

"Reggie, as the bean counter that you are, you will be so glad to know we will stop duplicating our buying because now we know exactly what we have. You know, I know that First Baptist down the street could use these supplies for their Mother's Day Out program. Do you care if I call Helen over there? She is a wonderful woman and runs a great program for kids there."

"Amy, wow, this is great! I like to hear of anything that will help us be better stewards of what we have. Um … regarding Helen, well, I think we should give this equipment to one of our churches in the brethren, don't you? I mean we know for sure that *we* are at least preaching sound doctrine."

"Uh–oh. Well, I just figured we were all in God's family, and working toward the same efforts. If that is what you think we should do, I"ll …"

1. Have you had events in your community that allowed you to meet Christians from other church traditions? What was your experience?

2. Think about the church you attend or the church you grew up in? Did you sense from your denomination that they believed to have the best doctrine? How did this affect your view of other Christians?

3. Read Ephesians 4:1-6. What are some attitudes that can help us move toward biblical unity relationally?

4. Do you feel like you know how to define the Christian faith? What makes someone a brother or sister in Christ?

Real Life Lessons:

The history of the Christian church is full of heroes and heroines, thieves and murderers, martyrs and monks. Like it or not, all of Christendom share the same history. We cannot deny our bond, no matter how hard we try. We all need to take responsibility for the relational strife that still exists.

The Great Schism of 1054 was the first great split of the church, separating East from the West. Then in 1517, Luther posted his 95 Theses on October 31, marking the beginning of the Reformation, the next great rift in the church. Since then, we have actually thousands of Christian denominations on record. Sometimes churches split for noble reasons, sometimes for wrong, trivial reasons. Who is right, and who is wrong?

One thing can be observed. If we take an honest look at the various doctrines of each denomination, no one church has a market on sound doctrine. All of us are prone to error in some way. Each denomination brings a strength to the Body that is often lacking in another expression of Christianity. As Christians, we are all brothers and sisters in Christ and we should feel freedom to disagree on the nonessentials—those things that do not pertain to salvation, or the core beliefs of the historic Christian church. The essentials we can all embrace as followers of Christ, and

112

we should be able to recognize them. The Apostles' Creed came about around 700 AD to protect the church against heresy. Many churches recite it each week during worship. Its truth still today resounds the core beliefs of Christianity:

Apostles' Creed
"*I believe in God the Father almighty, creator of heaven and earth; And Jesus Christ, His only Son, our Lord, Who was conceived by the Holy Spirit, born of the Virgin Mary, suffered under Pontius Pilate, was crucified, dead and buried. He descended to hell, on the third day rose again from the dead, ascended to heaven, sits at the right hand of God the Father almighty, thence will come to judge the living and the dead; I believe in the Holy Spirit, the holy catholic Church, the communion of saints, the forgiveness of sins, the resurrection of the body, and the life everlasting. Amen.*"

In general in this postmodern era, we also see the church struggling with its identity, which also affects our pursuit of relational unity. Leaders across denominational lines are asking the same questions: Who are we? Should we try and be something else? And, are we really doing it right? Once again we tend to continue to come up with different answers. We have mega churches, mainline churches, Catholic churches, house churches, seeker-sensitive churches, emerging churches, and even churches who don't call themselves churches. Sometimes we separate not necessarily because of doctrine but because of preferences. This may not be a malicious divisiveness, but we can forget that there is a church down the road trying to bring people to Christ just like your own church. We need to remember our call to one another, as Jesus prayed that we would be one, just as He is One with His Father. Now that is close kin.

Remember God has laid a circle of freedom within Christianity.

Orthodox Christianity lays down a circle rather than a tiny dot. There should be freedom to express the same truth differently. Remember Jesus had very harsh words for the legalism among the religious leaders of His day. Relationships among Christians can be messy, but we should not give up this important fight. The world needs to see unified Christians working together, so that they, too, might believe.

Real Life Strategies:

* Don't focus on trying to pursue an institutional unity; rather, focus on relational unity.

* Avoid sectarian attitudes, such as believing your own particular church has a superior claim to represent the Body of Christ, minimizing other groups.

* Our differences should never be cause to stop loving one another (John 15:12).

* Go outside of your comfort zone and meet Christians from other denominations that you don't know much about.

* Do not pursue unity at the expense of truth. We are to be committed to both truth and love.

Real Life Wisdom:

A house divided cannot stand. —Abraham Lincoln

In essentials, unity, in nonessentials, liberty, in all things charity. —Melanchthon

114

Savvy Resources for Additional Study:
One Lord, One Faith
By Rex Koivisto (Eugene, OR: Wopf and Stock Publishers, 1989)

The Church: Contours of Christian Theology
By Edmund P. Clowney (Downers Grove, Ill: InterVarsity Press, 1995)

The Body
By Chuck Colson (Nashville: Word Publishing, 1992)

Brethren, if a man is overtaken in any trespass, you who *are* spiritual restore such a one in a spirit of gentleness, considering yourself lest you also be tempted.

Galatians 6:1

21.
HOW DO I SUBMIT TO LEADERSHIP I DON'T RESPECT?

Real Life Question:

Can I submit to church leadership that I do not necessarily respect or agree with on everything? How do I know when to address an issue that is wrong, or when to let it go?

Real Life Case Study:

Ted and his family had been members of their church for twenty years. Ted was just voted in as the newest elder and began to see some of the conflicts he would have to face. He longed for the days when he just served as a member.

Ted was appointed to several committees and began to work directly with Pastor Jerry, a new pastor on staff. He was one of the younger pastors and didn't always have the best listening skills. Ted really struggled with Pastor Jerry's attitude toward the seniors of the church. For Pastor Jerry, anything new and hip was where he wanted to be. He didn't seem to know that he had a responsibility to reach out to all generations as a shepherd of the church. Pastor Jerry didn't get along with most of the elders, and they all sort of just put up with his immaturity and his fits of anger. One morning before the service started, he screamed at the senior pastor, stomping on a pile of boxes, shouting, "Do I have to do everything around here?"

Ted began to get complaints from other seniors who said they were brushed aside when trying to talk with Pastor Jerry. He seemed to favor a few families and listen to their concerns, but he didn't seem to care about the vast majority of the congregation. Being a new elder, Ted was puzzled why this was allowed to continue, but was determined to bring up the issue at the next elder's meeting.

"Ted, we all know how Pastor Jerry is, and he has a lot of growing up to do. He is the son of one of our biggest givers and it is complicated," explained the chairman of the elders.

"Complicated? It isn't complicated to me. He is wounding many of our members and some are leaving because of his poor people skills. He walks around the church like it is his church, and I think he is in need of discipline. I can't tell you how many calls I've had from our members complaining about his poor pastoral care, and I've only been in office for a month."

"Well I just wonder if all of these people have confronted Pastor Jerry and talked with him one on one. I mean, I don't want to sound like we aren't willing to talk with him, but ... Okay, well, since you have a burden for this, will you meet with him?" asked Chairman Collins.

1. Church conflict that deals with leadership issues can be

terribly stressful. Have you been involved in conflict with leadership? Think of a situation where you found it difficult to respect those in authority. What was your response?

2. Read Matthew 18:15-20. Were the guidelines mentioned in these verses followed? What was the end result?

3. Have you ever left a church because you could not support the leadership? Looking back, do you feel like that was the wisest choice to make?

4. In what ways have you submitted to authority, even though it was very difficult to do so?

5. How do you think our relationship with God is affected by unresolved conflict with others?

Real Life Lessons:

When conflict arises with those that we view as shepherds and leaders of the church, our first inclination is to leave. In this age of consumerism, it is easy to just want to flee and find another place to worship. The church culture today has given us a lot of options to choose from and it can be tempting to just leave quietly out the back door. But often God calls us to be committed to hard relationships to cultivate a church that is healthy and safe for others.

Serving leadership that we do not respect can be a very difficult problem. Sometimes our feelings about a person in leadership are founded and there should be a confrontation of some sort, moving toward discipline and accountability. Other times, we have to acknowledge that we aren't going to like everyone who is a Christian in leadership and to let certain things go that do not affect the well being of the church body.

Knowing when to confront leadership and when to submit and serve is the wisdom we have to find. As servants of Christ, we do have to realize that many of the world's crises stem from rebellion against authority. We, too, can rebel against the authority God has placed in our lives and work against God's plan for His church.

We are called to respect those that are in roles of leadership, even when we don't necessarily like them. This does not mean we have to agree with all that they do, or submit to something who goes against Scripture. Ephesians 5:15-21 serves as a good guide in the attitude Christ would like us to have toward one another. Mutual submission on both sides is what God desires. Those in authority should submit to their flock and the flock should submit to the leadership of the church.

If leadership has sinned against you, according to Scripture, you must go to them personally. Everyone deserves a chance to be heard and to be restored. Sometimes our tendency can be to cut off someone before they even know there is a problem.

Even though you may not be a pastor or a visible leader in your church, as Christians, all of us are called to be servant leaders. Make sure you realize your responsibility to follow through relationally. When we are committed to each other and see ourselves as truly family, our churches become stronger and a better reflection of how Christ loves us.

Real Life Strategies:
* Realize the importance of good communication skills in resolving any conflict.

119

• Know your place and how God has positioned you to influence others.

• Know yourself. Do you have a tendency to be too critical? Be honest and pray to know when it is right to approach leadership.

• Don't leave a church just because conflict arises. The more involved we get with people and leadership, the more inevitable issues will arise. You may be someone God uses to promote positive change.

Real Life Wisdom:

For God, whenever it pleases him, changes the worst men into the best, engrafts the alien, and adopts the stranger into the church. And the Lord does this to frustrate men's opinion and restrain their rashness—which, unless it is checked, ventures to assume for itself a greater right of judgment than it deserves. –John Calvin

Savvy Resources for Additional Study:
Bold Love
By Dan Allender and Tremper Longman III (Colorado Springs: NavPress, 1992)

The Peacemaker
By Charles Spurgeon, http://www.peacemakers.net/peace/chs-peacemaker.htm

Kenneth Sande, Peacemakers Ministries offers helps in dealing with church conflict.
www.peacemakers.net

Thomas said to Him, "Lord, we do not know where You are going, and how can we know the way?" Jesus said to him, "I am the way, the truth, and the life. No one comes to the Father except through Me."
John 14:5-6

22.
HOW DO I RECOGNIZE HERESY?

Real Life Question:
How can I recognize a religious predator?

Sometimes it is hard to know if someone is a Christian or not. Christianity has taken on a broader understanding and in a pluralistic society, religious predators can blur the lines. How can we know if someone might be spiritually dangerous to listen to?

Real Life Case Study:
Kristy found herself going to a chiropractor that she really liked, and he said he was a Christian, which was an added plus. She was finding benefit from her treatments and planned to attend one of his exercise classes.

"Okay, class. I want to teach you a Taoist technique to help you press through the pain," explained Dr. Miller.

121

Kristy hesitated and looked around. She wasn't sure if she had ever heard anything about Taoism, but became uncomfortable with the class. She decided to sit out the rest of the class and observe everyone.

After class, Dr. Miller approached her intently. "Kristy, I see that you didn't participate. Is something wrong?"

"Uh, well . . . yes. I'm just confused a bit. I don't want to be rude or sound intolerant, but I'm a Christian and …"

"I am too, Kristy. But there isn't anything wrong with borrowing techniques from other sources of spiritual wisdom. You know our body is very tied to healthy expressions of spirituality."

"Well, I just need to study Taoism a bit before I … you understand, right?"

"Just know I would never do anything to harm you."

1. Have you found yourself confused with religious labels? Has someone said they were a Christian and then you discovered they believed differently than you?

2. Write out your definition of a Christian. Did you find it hard to define?

3. The New Age movement began in the 1960s when many people were turning to Eastern religions to fill the void they felt, which ultimately says that we all can be gods ourselves. New Age is a worldview that is prevalent in society. Can you see how it has crept into many facets of our society, even the church?

4. Describe an encounter with someone who turned out to be a religious predator. What was your response to them? Were you able to recognize how it was inconsistent with the Christian faith?

5. Read Ephesians 4:14-15 and 2 Timothy 4:2-5. How can we be prepared to give a biblically sound answer for our faith?

Real Life Lessons:

Christians today are often pegged as being intolerant and hostile toward other faiths. Therefore, we often feel the pressure to be overly accommodating when we are confronted with an expression of spirituality that is contrary to the Christian faith.

Oftentimes a religious predator will offer us something that we need, whether it is health, money, or companionship. They may look to where a person may be vulnerable in hopes of enticing them toward what their truth has to offer. Naively, we can think that we are safe if someone claims to love God. Christians need to be alert in realizing that people are making up their own religions, even in Christian circles.

The New Age Movement can be the most deceiving in that this worldview would usually tolerate a Christian influence that could be practiced in addition to incorporating New Age thought. For example, you may meet a Baptist girl who also goes for tarot card readings, only they are called "angel cards." This seems less offensive, but it is still a form of spirituality that is in opposition to the Christian faith. We can find subtle ways in which other religious practices are rubbing off on some of those in the pews.

First, if you have concern about someone's religious beliefs, find out exactly what they believe about Jesus. For a true Christian, Jesus Christ is the only way a person can be saved. Many religions would acknowledge that Jesus was a good man, but would deny that He was fully God. Some would acknowledge His moral teachings, but deny that He came to save the world. A Christian can prevent falling prey to heresy by knowing what Jesus someone is talking about. The Jesus of the Bible was fully God and fully man. He was born of a virgin, died on a cross, and was raised from dead in order that we might be saved from sin. Invariably a religious predator may put something on equal footing with Jesus.

Another thing to look for is any manipulative or fear tactics a person uses to win you over. They may say, "Well, you can't experience the fullness of your faith unless you add this teaching." Be careful of anything that is added as truth that is not found in the Bible. Any "sacred" text or teaching that is not found within orthodox Christianity should be dismissed as authoritative.

Also, be leery of anyone that would exalt themselves to all-knowing or as someone you must follow to get answers about life. If you sense a person is trying to control how you think or act, this is a clear indication that it is out of line with Christian theology. The Bible tells us that where the Spirit of the Lord is, there is freedom.

Today, many Christians are first generation Christians and may not know a lot of basic doctrine that could equip them to better understand their faith. Take time to study if you find you don't have a good handle on all aspects of who Jesus is, or about sin, or the Trinity. This can help you recognize religious predators much more quickly and you can feel confident in your own beliefs and make them your own, not relying on what your spouse believes or your friends.

If you find yourself in doubt in joining in any exercise our practice someone offers, whether it is your doctor, your dentist, or your hairdresser, don't. Stand your ground and trust the Holy Spirit is guiding you.

Real Life Strategies:

• Be leery of anyone that adds something else to Christianity as a means to God.

• Be literate in the Bible. You don't have to know everything, but seek to know the fundamentals of the Christian faith well.

• Don't be afraid to be labeled intolerant. Christianity is not inclusive of other faiths as being a valid way to God.

• Make a point to try and expose any false teachings the predator may present to you as truth. You may be able to use simple reasoning toward the true expression of Christianity.

• Predators may attempt to doing very good deeds, tending to the poor, reaching out to the sick. This does not make them Christians.

Real Life Wisdom:

The less reasonable a cult is, the more men seek to establish it by force.—Jean Jacques Rousseu

Preach the word! Be ready in season and out of season. Convince, rebuke, exhort, with all longsuffering and teaching. For the time will come when they will not endure sound doctrine, but according to their own desires, because they have itching ears, they will heap up for themselves teachers; and they will turn their ears away from the truth, and be turned aside to fables. —The Apostle Paul

Saavy Resources for Additional Study:
Handbook of Christian Apologetics
By Peter Kreeft (Downers Grove, IL: InterVarsity Press 1994)

Christian Research Institute
www.equip.org
Hank Hanegraaff

Basic Christianity
By John Stott (Downers Grove, Ill: InterVaristy Press, 1971)

PROBLEMS AT WORK

> Yet in all these
> things we are
> more than
> conquerors
> through Him
> who loved us.
> **Romans 8:37**

23.

HOW CAN I BEAT TEMPTATION?

Real Life Question:

How do I overcome a self-defeating temptation?

Everyone has been tempted at one time or another. Temptations can come when we least expect it, and we can find ourselves blindsided by the force and pull that they can present. How can we best resist falling into sinful choices?

Real Life Case Study:

Scenario #1: Lynn loves to shop. She knows her husband is the bean counter in the family and frowns on any trips to the mall. Every once in a while she finds herself having to travel for work. As soon as she steps off the plane, the urge to shop overtakes her. She often will try and fly a day early so she has time to hit her favorite spots. She always ends up spending more than she intended and feels that she does have a problem with just feeling the thrill of a new purchase. She finds herself avoiding price tags, and saying to herself, "I want what I want."

Scenario #2: Josh is extremely introverted. He has struggled with exerting energy in relationships and finds himself much more fascinated with technology. He escapes onto his computer after dinner most every night. Emily has been very vocal about her frustration and Josh ignores her pleas for more communication from him.

One night Josh realizes that he really is emotionally starved for human contact. Emily is asleep and he finds himself in a chat room with an interesting lady. She seems to be fascinated with Josh's knowledge about computers. Soon Josh finds himself chatting every night, communicating like he hasn't done with Emily in over a year. They soon plan to meet.

Scenario #3: Brandon is successful business executive who travels about four times a month. He doesn't mind the travel so much once he gets there and is working, but at times he resents being away from home, wondering if this is the best thing for his marriage.

To justify his long days of work, he opts for a nicer hotel and a little more posh restaurant than the last trip. Brandon finds that he is becoming intrigued with finding the most comfortable places in each city to fill the void he feels away from his wife. Each expense report he feels out seems to get a little more expensive each time. Soon his conscience is bothering him, but no one in accounting seems to care, so why not?

1. Think about a temptation that you are currently struggling with. Have you found ways to resist? Explain.

2. Read Genesis 2:16-17; 3:1-13. How did Satan skillfully tempt Eve? How does he skillfully know how to tempt you?

3. What is it that lies at the core of all temptation?

4. How does temptation make us doubt the power of God at work in us?

Real Life Lessons:

We live in an age that resoundingly says, "More is always better." This could mean more stuff, more power, more food, more sex, more popularity. The number of temptations we may have in a day can be overwhelming. Christians today find themselves in compromising situations, sometimes innocently and sometimes intentionally. To avoid falling into a sinful lifestyle, a wise Christian makes conscious efforts to devise a plan.

To help you avoid temptation, it is imperative to have a solid understanding of the meaning of life. Theoretically, Christians know that we are not what we own, yet the debt we have says we do not practice that belief. Theoretically Christians know that infidelity is wrong, yet statistics prove that we are breaking our wedding vows. Why are we failing at resisting temptation? If we realize we are not meant for this life alone, the way we live and the temporal pleasures have a way of taking the back seat to the divine calling before us. A savvy Christian realizes that nothing in this world can satisfy what we really are longing for—our eternal home. Without careful reflection on what life is all about, Christians can easily follow the advice of our world that tells us over and over, "It's okay, indulge."

Most of us are tempted by different things. Some people can look at a pie and take or leave it. Another wants to order two more. One man may find real temptation to be found on the Internet, and another would rather just sleep the day away. To beat temptation, first a Christian must own up to his or her weaknesses and have the courage to look at himself or herself honestly. James says, "Anyone who listens to the word but does not do what it says is like a man who looks at his face in a mirror and after at himself, goes away and immediately forgets what he looks like. But the man who looks intently into the perfect law that gives freedom, and continues to do this, not forgetting what he has heard but doing it—he will be blessed in what he does" (James 1:23-25 NIV).

Once you are acquainted with your temptations, figure out when they are hardest to resist. Is it when you are lonely, away from home? Is it when you are mad at your spouse and you want revenge? Perhaps your temptation is even rooted in your disappointment with God. If you cannot seem to trace when you are inclined to be tempted, prayerfully ask God to show you.

The church has recognized the seven deadly sins to be: lust, gluttony, greed, laziness, wrath, envy, and pride. Some temptations may include a little of each. To name them can also help us to pray more effectively about them and be quicker to recognize weak moments. Much has been written on these sins through the history of the church and if you find yourself identifying with any one in particular, the more you understand the core issues in your heart, the more equipped you will be at overcoming them.

In avoiding temptation, Jesus Himself knew how difficult it could be as He took on human flesh and was tempted in every way that we are. The Christian life was not meant to be lived out alone. A practice of confession among good, trusted Christian friends can also serve as a preventative. Having a couple friends faithfully praying for you can make all the difference in the world. Some days we may feel stronger than others. On the weak days, we need to feel freedom to rely on others who can point us to God.

Real Life Strategies:
* Take a moment to examine any hidden sins that you have kept from your spouse. Ask God to give you the courage to expose this area and pray together about it.

• Make note of your biggest temptation right now. Seek out godly counsel if you find you are unable to resist making sinful choices.

• If you feel you are about to give in, think of those you love and how it may affect them, and how it will affect your relationship with God.

• Do not buy into the lie that you cannot overcome a temptation that is a struggle. God is bigger than any temptation.

• Make a point to meditate faithfully on God's word, especially pertaining to your area of struggle. Remember David's words, "Your word I have hidden in my heart, that I might not sin against You." (Psalm 119:11)

Real Life Wisdom:

A silly idea is current that good people do not know what temptation means. This is an obvious lie. Only those who try to resist temptation after five minutes simply does not know what it would have been like an hour later. That is why bad people, in one sense, know very little about badness. They have lived a sheltered life by always giving in. We never find out the strength of the evil impulse inside us until we try to fight it: and Christ, because He was the only man who never yielded to temptation, is also the only man who knows to the full what temptation means—the only complete realist.–C.S. Lewis

Savvy Resources for Additional Study:
Screwtape Letters By C.S. Lewis
Confessions By St. Augustine

And whatever you do, do it heartily, as to the Lord and not to men, knowing that from the Lord you will receive the reward of the inheritance; for you serve the Lord Christ.
Colossians 3:23-24

24.
HOW SHOULD I DEAL WITH CONFLICT IN THE WORKPLACE?

Real Life Question:

Most people at work know I'm a Christian, but I struggle with confronting people when I feel like something is unfair or not ethical. How do I learn to better deal with conflict?

When working with people, Christian or non-Christian, conflict is inevitable. Most people naturally want to avoid conflict and complain to the wrong people or ignore that there is a real problem. What can we do as Christians to try and better handle conflict?

Real Life Case Study:

Stacie had ten projects pending and couldn't seem to get a hold of her boss. She couldn't move forward without his approval and was getting concerned that everything was about to fall apart. Her team had worked overtime for the past six months, and she did not want to let them down. Phil hadn't returned her phone calls or her e-mails for several days. He had flex hours and no one, not even his assistant, knew what his schedule was for the week. Stacie knew that many of her clients and team members were waiting to hear from her and she could not place anything on hold and make the proposed print deadlines.

Finally, she gets a message from Phil's assistant, saying he would be in over the lunch hour to get caught up on everything. Stacie plans to skip lunch and wait for him to make sure everything was on schedule.

Unfortunately, Phil never showed up and Stacie was left with a slew of calls to make to those who were waiting for the go ahead. Stacie didn't know who to talk to, but she knew this problem was a pattern and she could not continue to work under these conditions. She wondered if she should turn him into Human Resources, but knew she probably should talk with him first.

She had made up excuses for Phil before, but people were starting to catch on that someone was not following through with promises. Later that afternoon, his assistant relayed a message to Stacie that she was to make up a story as to why their vendors needed to give them more time. She was tired of covering up for him, and knew she had compromised. Stacie knew that her business ethics were higher than her boss's but was not sure if she should tell her superior how to run the department. Yet at some level, she knew she had to confront Phil, or just leave.

1. Having a conflict with someone at work, whether a fellow coworker or your boss, can be one of the most difficult situations. Have you ever had to confront a superior at work? A coworker? What was the hardest issue to confront?

2. How should a Christian view confrontation? What examples do we have of how Jesus dealt with conflict with others?

3. How might Stacie show integrity in her difficult situation?

4. Read Colossians 3:22-25. Do you think Scripture teaches us to submit to authority, even if someone wants us to go against our own moral convictions?

Real Life Lessons:

Christians sometimes make the mistake of thinking that work is just a paycheck. This is a wrong attitude and can explain why we often aren't willing to confront problems on the job because we view it as just a job, rather than work we do for the Lord.

You may feel like you are the only Christian and misunderstood by most, and perhaps you are afraid your job might be on the line if you were to stand up for what is right. However, as Christians we know that God is our provider, not our boss, or the company we work for. We cannot live for the approval of our supervisor and cower to things that are dishonoring to God.

At the same time, we do not have to behave self-righteously when we are confronted with conflict. We don't have to respond accusatorily. "I'm a Christian, how could you possible think I would lie for you?" There are ways to point out truth and avert others to what is right, focusing on better choices rather than just dwelling on all what is wrong. People deserve to be treated with respect, even though they may be the cause of the conflict.

The worst thing an employee can do is ignore conflict. Our human tendency can be to complain to those that have nothing to do with the situation, or keep it inside. As Christians we do have a moral obligation to try live out our moral convictions, even if it means we make a few enemies along the way. When we ignore bad, the tendency is for an environment to move toward rewarding "bad" behavior and punishing good behavior. When we ignore sin or a conflict, we are displaying a casualness toward God's laws, which benefit everyone. Christians sometimes believe that being "nice" means ignoring the bad business practices in someone else. But this is actually a selfish attitude, and there are some battles in the workplace God does want us to fight. Conflict can reveal our true character and how we respond in a crisis.

Real Life Strategies:

- If you are facing a work conflict, reflect on what you believe the source of the problem is. Is it relational? Is it a structural problem? Determine who you should go to in moving toward resolve.

- Pray for godly courage to live out your moral convictions at work.

- Resolving conflict usually takes confrontation, but we can speak truth in love and change our workplace for the better.

- Accept that conflict is often necessary to bring about positive change. View conflict as a way for you to grow spiritually and as a professional in the workplace.

- Remember living out your moral convictions may not result in any earthly reward or the desired outcome. Be strong and resolved to please God, not man.

Real Life Wisdom:

If *we are growing, we are always going to be out of our comfort zone.* –John Maxwell

Savvy Resources for Additional Study:

The 360 Degree Leader: Developing your Influence from Anywhere in the Organization
By John Maxwell (Nashville: Thomas Nelson, 2006)

The Making of a Leader
By Dr. Robert Clinton (Colorado Springs: NavPress, 1988)

Let nothing be done through selfish ambition or conceit, but in lowliness of mind let each esteem others better than himself. Let each of you look out not only for his own interests, but also for the interests of others.

Philippians 2:3-4

25.
WHAT IS THE BEST WAY TO GET ALONG?

Real Life Question:

I work with some very difficult people, and it seems like my efforts to promote teamwork don't work with them. How can I get along with difficult people?

Real Life Case Study:

"I've had it! Either he goes, or I go. No one could pay me enough to keep putting up with his bad attitude. He is impossible to work with."

"Clara, I understand what you mean, but we just ask that you persevere a bit longer. I'm going to talk with Rick. He knows he is a problem."

"I just don't know if I can hang on any longer. He is making my job miserable and I spend way too much time trying to get the simplest of tasks done. Because of him, I am unable to do my job well anymore."

Rick was a problem for many employees at CompuTech. Because of his own low self-esteem, he would often lash out at others trying to compensate for his lack of confidence. He was known for his sharp tongue and unpredictable mood swings. Not many were willing to take time to get to know him as a person and find out what was really going on in his life.

Rick actually was taking care of his mother who had terminal cancer. He also had recently gone through a divorce and there wasn't much good happening in his personal life. The stress in his life was off the charts. Work was really all he had, and he was about to lose his job.

1. Have you ever worked with a "Rick"? How did you deal with the situation?

2. If you were Rick's boss, how would you manage the relational conflicts?

3. Read Luke 14:13-21; James 2:8-9. Jesus had a special place in His heart for the needy. Reflect on what these passages have to offer in dealing with difficult people.

4. Why do you think most Christians give up when working with difficult people? Think about someone who did not give up on you and persevered in your relationship. How did that person's love change you?

Real Life Lessons:

In God's economy, relationships come first. This means we should be committed to those God places in our path, whether we like a certain person or not. It is easy, especially in the workplace, to wish someone away. But God may have wisely placed a difficult person in your path for reasons you may not know.

Initially, we tend to think that a difficult person may need to learn something from us, and that well may be true. However, we also may need to realize they may indeed be God's gift to us for a season, to grow us. This can be hard to digest if the person is obstinate, ugly, and just downright mean at times. But God always sees the bigger picture, and His ways are higher than our own ways.

Humility is very important to display when working with difficult people. A person can quickly sense if you respect them or not. Philippians 2 is a great chapter to read on what true humility looks like. You might have to give up your own rights to serve someone. Jesus was the supreme example of a humble servant, as He gave up His rightful throne to take on human flesh. God may have a lesson on pride through a difficult relationship. Be open to God's discipline.

As Christians, we also need to realize that we are blessed by God. The benefits of having a relationship with Jesus are endless. Many people need to know that they really do have a hope and a future. We will encounter many frustrated, angry, unfulfilled people in this world, whether fighting traffic or on the job. Our conventional wisdom tells us if someone has done something wrong to us, we should just fight back. Jesus said if someone strikes you, offer the other cheek. The dignity and worth of another person transcends their wrongdoing in the kingdom of God. But there will be times when we do have to confront bad behavior, but never cutting off hope that a person can change.

If you are faced with working with a difficult personality, commit to praying for that person for thirty days. There isn't anything magical about thirty days, but it is a good period of time to observe how your prayers may benefit them and benefit your own attitude towards them. You may find yourself amazed at the change in your relationship, and the change in yourself.

Real Life Strategies:

• See yourself as a servant and be willing to go the extra mile at work, even it is for an enemy.

• Pray for an extra measure of discernment when dealing with a difficult person. God will be faithful to show you the good things about them if you take time to seek them out.

• Try and understand your coworker's perspective, however irrational it may be to you.

• Sharpen your listening skills.

• Seek out a mentor you respect whom you have observed works well with difficult people. Ask for advice.

Real Life Wisdom:

Love is the only force capable of transforming an enemy into friend. –Martin Luther King, Jr.

Listen to your enemies, for God is talking. –Jewish Proverb

Savvy Resources for Additional Study:
Read Philippians 2

The Peacemaker: A Biblical Guide to Resolving Personal Conflict
by Ken Sande (Grand Rapids: Baker Books, 2003)

Love Your Enemies
By John Piper

For we are His workmanship, created in Christ Jesus for good works, which God prepared beforehand that we should walk in them.
Ephesians 2:10

26.
HOW CAN I BE A BETTER EMPLOYEE WHEN I HATE WORK?

Real Life Question:

I really hate my job. I am trying to be grateful, but it is so hard to wake up in the morning and be excited about the day. How can I try and be a better employee, even though I continually live for the weekends, and dread my job?

Not everyone has a job that is fulfilling, and sometimes our circumstances require that we work in a place that feels like a dead end. Why we end up at a certain job can be difficult to figure out and God's silence on the matter can be deafening.

Real Life Case Study:

Joe had always been the provider of the family. His company went through a significant downsizing and had to lay off half of their engineers. The job had been good to them, and he was sad to leave.

Weeks passed and his severance package had run out. After sending resume after resume in his related field, he began to grow uneasy and unsure of what God had for him. His wife, Mary, had her nursing degree and had stayed home with their daughter Sarah since she was born. As they discussed their situation, they determined that it would be wise to see if Mary could get a nursing job, while he took care of Sarah.

Mary found a job right away and eased back into the workforce quite easily. The transition was much harder for Joe. He found a part-time job loading trucks nearby. He found himself wondering why he had gone to college and if this was his future. He couldn't see why God would lead him to a dead-end job. The days were miserable and he felt the mindless work to be a kind of prison. The language he had to put up with and the lazy coworkers made his day seem like wasted, futile time. Slowly, Joe slipped into a depression.

Joe knew God must be doing a work in him, but he still felt lost and alone while he was at work, just not fitting in. He didn't want to fall into thinking he was better than anyone else. Finally, he realized he needed to pray for God's perspective.

The next morning at 5:00 a.m. Joe got up as usual, but he stopped by the living room window. He had never noticed such a beautiful sunrise.

1. Think of a job that you had to endure—perhaps it is the one you are in. How did you, or how do you now, persevere?

2. What are some positive things about the job you can think about? What did you learn about God during this time?

3. Has God provided any unexpected blessing that through the process of enduring you would not have received otherwise?

4. Read part of Joseph's story in Genesis 39. Joseph experienced many injustices in his life, which included time in prison. In what ways can you relate to his life?

5. Has God given you favor with those you work with that you cannot explain?

Real Life Lessons:

Not everyone is blessed with a job they love. Most everyone has had to endure an unfulfilling job full of drudgeries for a time. You may be one who is really struggling in this area and wondering why God will not relieve you from this assignment.

Having a proper perspective can really help you be a better employee. Joseph is a great example of this. He was able to define his life as an opportunity to bring glory to God. Even though he experienced trials that could make any man bitter, he chose to see these setbacks as God's sovereign hand at work. Joseph believed that through his circumstances he could be best used as God's instrument. This is a hard lesson for those of us who are used to instant success.

Maybe your work feels to you like a prison. All the more reason you might relate to Joseph. Though Potiphar's wife schemed against Joseph and had Joseph wrongfully thrown in prison, Joseph did not live as a defeated man. While he was in prison, he found favor with the warden, who made him responsible for all those there with him. Even in the negative environment of prison, the lowest in society, God was at work. Joseph was given success at all he did while he graciously served his sentence. Genesis 39:23 says that the Lord was with Joseph and gave him success in whatever he did.

When we realize we are not alone, our job can take on a new dimension. God is not wasteful and knows exactly where we should be and for how long. And, if you are in a place that you are not supposed to be, He will be faithful to reveal that to you. Though it may feel like He is not present in our situation, He promises us that He is.

Think for a moment about the job you hate. Does it allow you more time to pray for your boss while you are doing a mindless task, like making copies, loading boxes, or filing? What are some of the perks of being bored at times or unchallenged? Perhaps that job has made you appreciate the people you work with, placing less focus on the bottom line—which is money in the world of business. Your job performance may even improve because you value the camaraderie that is there. You have begun to realize you aren't the only one just trying to endure.

Like nothing else, a difficult job can drive us toward God. He may be building your character and teaching you to slow down and wait on Him. You may be sent on assignment to share Christ with someone else, or maybe God has a friend that will end up being a life-long friend. God is all about relationships and will go to great lengths to accomplish His will through people. Don't be surprised to find the job you hate to be the biggest blessing in disguise.

Being a better employee may require the discipline of practicing the presence of God. Brother Lawrence, a Carmelite of the seventeenth century, wisely reminds us the value of realizing God is always present with us. Lawrence called himself "the lord of all pots and pans" in honor of his employment in the kitchen. He took his simple, menial work and turned it into "the sacrament of the present moment." As you are on the job, maybe it is here that you feel furthest away from His presence. But the truth He is always present with us, and by meditating on His love and His goodness, you may find it easier to recognize His nearness.

Most of us at some level find ourselves in a job devoid of glamour, prestige, or status. But God has given us all the same amount of time in a day to serve Him. Time is a sacred gift God has given us, and when we see each moment as an opportunity for God's will to be done here on earth, we can lift the drudgeries of the day confident that He has something eternal and lasting in mind.

Real Life Strategies:

- Don't compare your situation with those around you. God has given you assignments only you are to fulfill.

- Rest in God's sovereignty. He is at work on your behalf.

- Be thankful that He has given you an opportunity to work.

- If you find yourself unchallenged, look for ways to be challenged and prove to be someone your employers can trust.

Real Life Wisdom:

There is not in the world a kind of life more sweet and delightful, than that of a continual conversation with God. Those only can

comprehend it who practice and experience it. – Brother Lawrence "Commit to the Lord whatever you do, and your plans will succeed." (Proverbs 16:3 NIV)

Savvy Resources for Additional Study:
Practicing the Presence of God
By Brother Lawrence (New York: Doubleday, 1977).

Redeeming the Time: A Christian Approach to Work and Leisure
By Leland Ryken (Grand Rapids: Baker, 1995).

27.
IS THERE A DIFFERENCE BETWEEN MY CAREER AND MY CALLING?

Therefore do not be ashamed of the testimony of our Lord, nor of me His prisoner, but share with me in the sufferings for the gospel according to the power of God, who has saved us and called us with a holy calling, not according to our works, but according to His own purpose and grace which was given to us in Christ Jesus before time began.
2 Timothy 1:8-9

Real Life Question:
What is the difference between career and calling?

You know, I hear a lot people say they feel called to be a dentist or a doctor. But I can't say I feel called to my full-time job. Am I wrong to keep a job that I don't necessarily feel called to do?

Sometimes when we hear the word *calling* we think of God audibly telling us to "Go, ye therefore." How do we know what our calling is and if it has anything at all to do with our job?

Real Life Case Study:
Keith had served faithfully in the Air Force for twenty-

five years. He was thankful for the benefits it had given him educationally and the provision it gave his family. Most of the time, he didn't enjoy his assignments. He encountered many disappointments over the years, and his family moved every few years, sacrificing a lot relationally. Keith could point to moments in his career when he knew God used him in a special way, but every day wasn't like that. It usually was when he was teaching cadets and when he had opportunities to share his faith.

Keith was looking forward to retirement. He was still young and could afford to move into a new career of his choice and not worry about salary. After prayerful consideration, he kept finding himself thinking about teaching. He went to a small Bible college and found that he had a great desire to invest in the minds of young people, as so many professors had molded him years ago. The idea of raising his family in a small town had great appeal after they had lived in many major cities of the world. As he prayed, the sense of calling to teach intensified and he knew God was speaking. All of a sudden he realized his military career was the resource God would use to allow him to pursue what he was really passionate about.

1. Do you have a sense of calling outside of your occupation?

2. What are some of the ways your job allows you to pursue your life-purpose calling?

3. Read Hebrews 11. Think about the heroes of our faith and how they lived outside of the status quo, living in complete devotion to their calling to follow the Lord. How does the passage encourage you in career and calling?

4. Do you feel like you have a clear understanding of your life's calling or are you still grappling with what God has for your life?

Real Life Lessons:

When we meet someone for the first time we naturally ask, "So what do you do?" Our culture often views what we do as who we are. A job is often a place where we find significance or are made to feel productive. If we are fortunate, our occupation is something where we can steward our natural gifts and our spiritual gifts.

But calling is something that is much bigger than a career. Take for example the Apostle Paul. He knew his ultimate calling was to Christ and to spread the Gospel to Jews and Gentiles. His job did not define him. His calling was with God first. His giftedness and skills were not exhausted in the making of tents. His destiny did not lie in his parents' wishes for his life, or with the Pharisees, or the demands of the Greek culture.

When we accept the ultimate calling, which is to follow Christ, we then are able to pursue our individual calling with a balanced, godly perspective. Our life calling comes when we have wholeheartedly said, "I will follow You, Lord." In response to giving Him our lives, we are able to know our life-purpose calling, which can only be partially fulfilled on the job. Our life-purpose permeates every moment of the day.

There is a tendency to hyper-spiritualize our calling at times. Some look for a sign from God for every task they choose to do always asking, "Was I called to this job?" When others confess they do not have a sense of calling in this way, they tend to feel left out or not used by God. But the New Testament does not give us examples of people necessarily called to a paid occupation.

As Christians, it is also important to remember not to see ourselves solely in light of our giftedness and elevate it beyond what God intended. We are stewards of the gifts He has given us, and they are not for us to determine how we use them apart from God. Selfishly, we can steward them to serve ourselves, and that is not following God's call. We may find that our spiritual gifts and natural gifts are hardly used at work.

Work, for most of us, is a responsibility we bear that often does not match the calling God has placed on our lives. God fully knows how He created us and who we really are. A job can only define us by what we do and how we perform. God sees and knows us at the core of our being, which transcends occupation. For most it is difficult to find a clear connection between calling and work.

Yet we know our work can glorify God when we do it well. God uses our time on the job to afford us time to free us to pursue our life-purpose calling. If you find your work unfulfilling at different levels, you are not alone. Most people don't.

Our calling can be difficult to discern at different times in life. But our calling is with us throughout our lives. An occupation will move us toward retirement after so many years of work, but the calling on our life is for a lifetime.

Real Life Strategies:
• Realize that your job does not define who you are.

- You are more than your gifts, which are given to you by God. They don't belong to you, but rather are to be stewarded to glorify God.

- Trust God to reveal His plan for you, whether it is pursuing a different job or pursuing the call He has on your life.

Real Life Wisdom:

If you can tell where you got the call of God and all about it, I question whether you have ever had a call. The call of God does not come like that, it is much more supernatural. The realization of it in a man's life may come with a sudden thunder clap or with a gradual dawning, but in whatever way it comes it comes with the undercurrent of the supernatural, something that cannot be put into words.—Oswald Chambers

Savvy Resources for Additional Study:

The Call: Finding and Fulfilling the Central Purpose of Your Life
By Os Guinness (Nashville: Word Publishing, 1998)

Why Work? Careers and Employment in Biblical Perspective
By John Bernbaum and Simon Steer (Grand Rapids: Baker, 1987)

To Be Told: Know Your Story, Shape Your Future by Dan Allender (Waterbrook Press, Colorado Springs, 2005)

There are many plans in a man's heart, nevertheless the LORD's counsel—that will stand.
Proverbs 19:21

28.
HOW DO I MAKE A BIG MOVE PROFESSIONALLY AND KNOW IT IS RIGHT?

Real Life Question:

How do I make a big career move when I feel like God is being silent on the matter? How can I know if it is a wise choice?

Sometimes it is hard to discern if we should take a promotion and relocate or if we should stay where we are. Both have pros and cons. After praying about, you don't sense God is swaying you really toward one or other. How can we know we are making the right decision?

Real Life Case Study:

Tom was up for a good promotion. He had worked hard to be recognized by his boss, sometimes sacrificing time with his family. The promotion would call for relocating and he knew that would be hard for his wife, Julie.

"Hey, Jules. Got some news."

"Yeah? What's up?"

"Well, Mr. Richardson called me in his office and said he had been very pleased with my managerial skills. He offered me a great new position, but it would mean relocating. What do you think?"

"Tom, that is so great your hard work is paying off . . . I just love it here, though. We finally have a church where we feel at home and such great friends. We'd be giving up a lot relationally. And, I always envisioned our kids growing up around their grandparents. Giving up family is huge."

"Yes, there would be a lot we'd be giving up."

"Tom, what do you think about moving?"

"Well, I don't like the idea. This really feels like home, but the opportunity professionally would be great . . .well, we don't have to answer right away."

1. Think about a time when you had to give up something to gain. Looking back, would you say you made the right decision for the right reasons?

2. Reflect on how you usually make decisions. Do you seek out counsel, or do you make decisions on your own?

3. Think about a time when you feel like you made a wrong decision. What lessons did you learn about yourself?

4. Read James 3:13-18. Consider a decision that you are faced with or may expect to face in the near future. Think about your decision in light of this passage. Write out your thoughts.

Real Life Lessons:

Decisions, decisions, decisions. We all have to make them each day of our lives. Some big, some small. As Christians, big and small decisions matter to God. If we are faithful with little, we can be trusted to be faithful with much. Small wise choices turn into bigger wise choices.

Career moves can be tricky, as a Christian should consider more than just how much money the job offers. *Does the job utilize what I feel God is calling me to do? How will the decision affect my relationship with God? Will I be able to still have quality time with family and friends?* These questions matter and will impact what decision seems wise. Rarely does God call us to accept a job just because it offers more money.

Realizing God's value system is different from the world's is key when making big decisions. God views career, money, and family much differently than our culture. Career is not synonymous with calling for God. Calling is something that we never retire from that goes well beyond the workplace. Money is not all-powerful as the world views it. Marriage is a sacred covenant, not a relationship of convenience. When we understand God's ways, we are better equipped to move toward His wise counsel.

After considering what God values, then consider your own motives. Would the decision benefit others besides you? Would the decision cause you to pursue selfish ambition? What good fruit might come from your decision to say yes? Will the decision ultimately draw you closer to God?

Prayer is a very important step in making a decision. God may or may not give you a specific answer. If you have given the decision prayerful consideration and are still unsure what He would have you do, trust the freedom He has given you. Think about the freedom a parent gives a child. A mother may allow her young son to play in his room how he chooses. She does not pick out every toy, or determine what games he will play. She just allows his personality to have the freedom to play as he wills within the boundaries of safety she has set. God's freedom is similar. He entrusts us to think and exercise our choice if the choice does not harm us. When He is silent, it does take a measure of faith to believe He trusts you to decide with the wisdom He has already revealed to you through His Word, godly counsel, and prayer.

As you look to make a big decision, be prepared to give up whatever God is asking of you. Most likely, a sacrifice will be involved. Be willing to leave open hands before the Lord, not holding on to anything too tightly other than Him. Remember, God always has your best interest at heart.

Real Life Strategies:

• Don't panic when you are faced with a big decision. Trust the Spirit is guiding you and is your Counselor.

• Examine your motives prayerfully.

• Ask yourself, "If more money weren't in the equation, would I still be interested in the opportunity?"

• Would the decision pull you away from what you feel God has called you to do with your life?

Real Life Wisdom:

If any of you lacks wisdom, let him ask of God, who gives to all liberally and without reproach, and it will be given to him. But let him ask in faith, with no doubting, for he who doubts is like a wave of the sea driven and tossed by the wind. For let not that man suppose that he will receive anything from the Lord; he is a double-minded man, unstable in all his ways. –James 1:5-8

Know that it's your decisions, and not your conditions, that determine your destiny. -Joyce Meyer

Savvy Resources for Additional Study:
Decision-Making and the Will of God: A Biblical Look at the Alternative View
By Garry Friesen (Multnomah, 1980.)

John Maxwell's leadership resources and articles can be found at www.injoy.com

> And let us not grow weary while doing good, for in due season we shall reap if we do not lose heart.
>
> **Galatians 6:9**

29.
WHY ARE CHRISTIANS THE HARDEST TO GET ALONG WITH AT WORK?

Real Life Question:

Why am I finding that Christians can be the hardest people to work with? It seems like most of my struggles tend to be with the ones who know better, yet choose bad behavior. I'm just tired of working with people that disappoint me.

The workplace can bring very diverse people together in sometimes very tight quarters with little or no breathing room. Often we spend more time with people at work than we do with our families. So when we find someone who shares our same faith and values, it can be very disheartening when their Christian witness disappoints us.

Real Life Case Study:

Jenny had mainly been employed by Christian organizations since she finished graduate school. To get through school, she did work retail and was thankful for the paycheck each week. But she felt God was calling her to ministry in some capacity. Unsure of the next steps, she decided to take a hike in the mountains and pray before making any big decisions. She did feel tempted to go back to her retail job and just forget the whole pursuit of full-time ministry work.

Jenny had a graduate internship under her belt and had worked for a church and two nonprofit ministries. Jenny didn't ever think she would feel so worn out so fast. She thought fresh air would rejuvenate her a bit. As she found a friendly path, she began to hike the trail full of determination as she thought about what might be her next ministry assignment. Thinking about the leadership she had worked for was her biggest struggle. The work was rewarding and the job positions themselves were wonderful opportunities. But she found herself longing for the bosses she had in the retail world, who weren't Christians. They seemed to be more honest and fair.

Painful memories surfaced as she thought about some of the hard times she had endured. Jenny remembered taking her first graduate internship feeling God had specifically led her to that church. She remorsefully thought about her boss, and the day she found out about the affair. Feelings of betrayal, disappointment, and distrust flooded over her heart once again. Yet, through the pain, she knew God had faithfully led her there. It was here she learned the truth about ministry and the truth about the human condition. Her idealistic dream about ministry was forever changed.

Jenny took a deep breath and lifted her head toward the peaceful sky. She was glad to feel the soft earth beneath her feet and hear the calming breeze that echoed around her thoughts. Somehow, she knew she would gather strength to look beyond the past few years. Like many times before, she told God of her disappointment in leadership. Never did she think someone in leadership would be hiding an affair while on a church staff. Never did Jenny think she would work for a Christian man who would ask her to lie to the ministry's board of directors. She just wasn't sure if she could work for one more Christian and expect to find Christian ethics being applied. Yet she was still inclined to hope ...

1. Have you been disappointed with Christian leadership or a Christian coworker? What lessons did you learn about relationships?

2. Why do you think Christians struggle with ethics in the workplace just as nonbelievers do?

3. Do you think your expectations of other Christians are realistic?

4. Read I Kings 19:1-18. When have you felt like giving up on people? Have you found yourself to the only one sticking up for what is right, even among Christians?

5. Elijah may have felt like his confrontation on Mount Carmel was supposed to bring about revival for the Israelites, and then was deeply disappointed when that didn't happen. When have you been gravely discouraged because your efforts did not bring about positive change?

Real Life Lessons:

Say you were to be president of a new nation and you were given hundreds of square miles to create an ideal society. You also had the power to choose those who would run the government.

161

And, to top it off, all citizens would be professing, strong Christians. How long do you think it would take before you encountered a problem?

The answer: not long at all. Why? Because sometimes we forget, even though we are Christians, that sin is still a problem. The Fall has affected us all, though we do have daily choices to say no to sin. Sometimes we forget all about the doctrine of sin.

You might be dealing with a lot more than trying to work with a grumpy, cantankerous Christian. Your problems with leadership may be much more serious and despairing. When we work for Christians or know one of our coworkers is a person of faith, our expectations can be unrealistic. Sometimes we place higher expectations on others morally than what we require of ourselves. As you encounter conflict, remember to be mindful of your conduct and what God requires of you first and foremost. Try and give the person the benefit of the doubt when at all possible. Look for opportunities to discuss the problems you see with respect and with honesty.

When there are serious sin issues involved, your choices may be to leave or be fired. Sometimes, even when practicing honest attempt toward resolution, if there is no repentance of wrong or an ability to see wrong, it's possible that you will not have the favorable outcome you desire. Realize that you may display the best Christian character possible when dealing with your coworker, but still the wrong behavior may continue. This is not a reason to give up or change your own moral convictions. In your last attempts to promote change, you may find yourself wanting to verbally attack someone or seek revenge. Remember, the biblical mandate we have to forebear. (Proverbs 25:15; Romans 2:4)

Be prepared to feel lonely and isolated when you are standing up for what is right. Remember Elijah also felt like he was the only one following God. But God showed him thousands who did not bow down to other idols. Prayerfully ask God to open your eyes to see the others around you who are also living by God's standards.

Above all, remember God is your defense. Read Psalm 37 as a reminder of where sin can lead a person. Sometimes it is hard to see the temporal advances of those that are not displaying Christian character, but there is a price that people pay to choose this way. Avoid the temptation of lowering your standards of conduct because of the reward you see others receiving.

If you have dealt with a string of negative experiences when working with Christians, make sure you do not let bitterness creep into your life. It is easy to be cynical and begin to always expect the worst. The good news is there is always hope and we should never cut someone off from the hope that they are called to in Christ.

Strive to be someone that people respect in the job force, even if your Christian ethics give you some enemies. Perhaps God is in the process of making you into a godly leader others will gladly follow.

Real Life Strategies:
- Don't expect Christians to be morally perfect.

- Expect more of yourself than from others.

- Realize that good leadership, even among Christians,

is rare. If have worked for a godly man or woman, count yourself very blessed.

* You may have to go through a very long line of bad leadership to find a positive experience. Use every negative example as a way to sharpen your own character.

Real Life Wisdom:
Some rise by sin, and some by virtue fall.—William Shakespeare

We read that we ought to forgive our enemies; but we do not read that we ought to forgive our friends. —Sir Francis Bacon

Savvy Resources for Additional Study:

The Making of a Leader
By J. Robert Clinton (Colorado Springs: NavPress, 1988).

Beyond Integrity
By Scott Rae (Grand Rapids: Zondervan, 1996)

Making the Most of Mistakes
By James D. Berkley (Nashville: Word, 1987)

Ethics
By Dietrich Bonhoeffer (New York: Simon & Schuster, 1995)

For I am not ashamed of the gospel of Christ, for it is the power of God to salvation for everyone who believes.

Romans 1:16

30.

HOW CAN I TALK ABOUT CHRISTIANITY IN A NON-THREATENING WAY AT WORK?

Real Life Question:

How can we share our faith with someone of another faith and dialogue in a way that is meaningful?

God isn't exactly the most popular person in our culture, and unfortunately the pressure to be politically correct is more the standard in the workplace than being committed to God and His Truth. If we aren't careful, we can live somewhere in the extremes of our options. Either we think we should confront a person at every moment with a verse of the Bible, or we live on the other side, where we feel we don't have a right to give our testimony of what God has done. Sharing our faith and dialoguing with a nonbeliever can be a paralyzing fear for many Christians, especially with those we work with forty plus hours a week who know our shortcomings.

We know it is wrong *not* to share our faith with others, but we also don't want a colleague telling HR that some suspect we belong to a cult because we love Jesus. Though on the job isn't always the most appropriate time, we do need to get beyond our politically correct loyalties that slam the doors shut. How can we share our Christian faith with someone of another faith and dialogue in a way that is meaningful? Being savvy requires that we know when and how to make the most out of every opportunity we are given.

Real Life Case Study:

Meg finds herself at the company office Christmas party. HR's social committee has arranged for assigned seating in hopes that employees will get to know those from other departments. Glancing at the unfamiliar name cards, she reluctantly sits and introduces herself to the gentleman next to her.

"Please to meet you, Meg. My name is Ramesh and my family moved here from India a few months ago to join the team here."

"Well, welcome to the office. I hope your first Christmas here is a special one."

"Oh, well I don't celebrate Christmas. I am Hindu. . . ."

Meg is at the right place and time to share what she believes to be true about her Christian worldview. She is in a friendly, relaxed environment just trying to know a coworker better. This is a great time to build a respectable relationship and dialogue about what matters to Ramesh. You don't have to be invasive when dialoguing about faith and differing worldviews. Most likely, you find conversation naturally flows toward what someone values and admires. A worldview is how we view life, which ultimately reveals how we view God. A Christian doesn't necessarily have to memorize the right verses of the Bible in order to share their faith effectively.

Look for moments that naturally lead to the big questions of life: Why am I here? What is my purpose? Is my life significant in the grand scheme of the universe? Think of all of God's natural laws that are undeniable that speak to a higher intelligence and purposeful, created order (Romans 1:20). As Christians, we believe that we are all created in the image of God and that all of humanity bears His image. Therefore, the nonbeliever and believer alike have a have the inherent desire to know Truth. To realize that we have more common desires and even fears about this life can remove barriers that Christians can put up before even trying. Dialoguing and trying to understand another worldview is really what you might call pre-evangelism and helps set the stage for someone to really share the Gospel with another.

1. Put yourself for a moment in Meg's situation. Write out how you would continue the conversation with Ramesh.

2. Think of some worldviews that you have encountered that clash with the Christian worldview.

3. What are some of the big questions about life that Christianity has answered for you personally? Identify some of these and prayerfully consider how to share these with someone you know who is in need of God's truth.

4. Read Acts 17:16-32. How did Paul use the truths about Creation in evangelizing his audience? What are some obvious truths that can be used as a point of dialogue to engage someone from another faith?

5. We are called to be witnesses, not necessarily eloquent evangelists. Take time to write out a 100-word testimony of what God has done for you. You may be surprised to find God may give you an opportunity share it sooner than you think.

Real Life Lessons:

Sometimes it is easy to think of our salvation as a done deal, a one-time event that is our ticket to heaven. Unfortunately, we can selfishly forget that our life in Christ is not the end of our story, but the beginning. Our salvation should impact all those who have a relationship with us. Our faith isn't supposed to be a privatized, selfish blessing. It should bless others.

We have often heard nonbelievers dismiss Christianity because you have to take a "leap of faith." But as we share our worldview with another person, they will find that Christianity engages the mind as well as the heart. God wants us to think deeply about our faith, as He is a God of intelligent design. When we begin to take time to unpack life benefits that come form the Christian faith, there is much there that can be talked about and actually tested in life. Take for example, the Ten Commandments. If we were to look at them, apart from any salvific good, anyone would agree that they create and protect families, neighbors, and a society. They protect freedom. Whether you know who God is, you can recognize how these laws can make a community safe. Our faith isn't blind, but rather it is informed by natural laws around us, the created order, and through God's special revelation, the Bible.

Think about the last time you were able to share God's truth with another person of another faith. If you do not have at least one friend that is not a Christian, pray for God to lead you someone to befriend. If you do have a friend that is a nonbeliever, ask the Lord to show ways to seize moments of opportunity this week to share your worldview.

Real Life Strategies:

- Be yourself when you are sharing your faith. You do not have to be an apologist to be qualified to evangelize someone else.

- Pray without ceasing. As you identify a moment of opportunity, pray for the Holy Spirit to give you confidence to share unashamedly what you believe in an honoring way.

- Don't wait until you have all answers. No one does, except God.

Real Life Wisdom:

Evangelism is just one beggar telling another beggar where to find bread. –D.T. Niles

It is right and inevitable that we should be much concerned about the salvation of those we love. But we must be careful not to expect or demand that their salvation should conform to some ready-made pattern of our own. –C.S. Lewis

Savvy Resources for Additional Study:
Search the Web and read about:
Naturalism
Existentialism
Nihilism
New Age

How Now Shall We Live? By Chuck Colson, (Wheaton: Tyndale, 1999)

Confessions and the City of God, St. Augustine

C.S. Lewis' Case for Christ, Art Lindsley

The Bible and Other Faiths: Christian Responsibility in a World of Religions,
By Ida Glaser (Intervarsity, 2005)

For we are His workmanship, created in Christ Jesus for good works, which God prepared beforehand that we should walk in them.
Ephesians 2:10

31.
HOW CAN I KNOW GOD'S PURPOSE AND CALLING FOR ME?

Real Life Question:

My life seems meaningless. Have I missed my calling and failed to see what God really wants me to do?

Everyone has a deep desire to live life with meaning and purpose. As God's most prized creation, He has designed for life to matter, and He has equipped us for every good work. But sometimes in the midst of cultural pressures, job security, and financial problems, our calling can seem to be fuzzy and we can find ourselves wondering if we took a wrong turn somewhere along the way. Finding what our calling is in life can be a lifelong quest. Do you feel like you have asked God to show you His desires for your life?

Real Life Case Study:

Don has been in corporate America for over twenty-five years. He is close to retirement and if he endures his job for just three more years, he won't have to worry about the family's income and will get a great benefit package.

But Don recently went for his check-up and the doctor said he must decrease his stress level and get his blood pressure down. Don is gearing up for employee reviews and he knows his boss is pressuring him to lay off twenty key positions. He knows some of the circumstances of his team. Judy is a single mom, supporting four children; Sam has been a faithful employee for years, but corporate is saying his job should be outsourced; Dale is always positive about whatever is dropped on his plate, but now he is going to have twice the workload with the new demands. Don finds himself wondering why he has given his life to this company, stuck in a job that doesn't seem to use all of his gifts.

If Don could turn back time, he would go back to pastoring. He was a youth pastor for a time, but was scared he couldn't offer his family financial security, so chose the corporate world reluctantly. Though he has made a great living and provided well for his family, he has missed ministry ever since he left.

Some are fortunate to love their job, which is a big part of their purpose and calling. But many find their work to be the most unfulfilling, drudgerous part of their lives. How can we know what our purpose is for sure? What does God really want us to know about our purpose and calling as Christians?

1. Reflect on your own life. Do you have a sense of what you believe God wants you to do with your life?

2. Have you gone through a period in your life where you wondered if you missed God's best for you? Explain.

3. Read Jeremiah 29:11. How have God's plans for your life proved to be better than your own?

4. Read Psalm 139. Reflect on God's perspective of you. How does His detailed acquaintance with you give purpose to your life?

5. Think for a moment how the dreams of others may have clouded your perspective of what your calling is.

Real Life Lessons:

It is easy to feel stuck. Maybe you feel like trying to define your call is the cruel riddle of life. Perhaps you are frustrated with where your heart wishes it were and where you actually are in life. As Christians, we have the hope of being first called to be Christ's ambassadors (2 Corinthians 5:18-21). We have been called to the ministry of reconciliation, sharing our faith with others. This is the most important call of all. How we can most effectively go about this task is the question we should pursue.

In our own personal search for significance and purpose, finding out who we really are isn't always a straightforward process. We have a tendency to measure our worth based upon our basket of rewards or promotions. But calling has little to do with earthly measurement and everything to do with who God designed you to be, which is more than what you do for a living. More importantly, we must understand fully that we are not just called to go do, but we are called to a person—to Someone. We are not first called to do some special task or make some stride in history but to God alone first. Everything else flows out of this relationship.

Deep in our inmost parts, we all want to find a purpose, to live for something that is bigger than ourselves. Today when we talk about purpose, we often pull out a spiritual gifts test and think that is all there is to it. Such assessments of self are helpful tools, but God created us with great complexity and our gifts may change as we go through life. When we truly find our calling, purpose in life is found at the deepest level and we feel fulfilled. Os Guinness defines calling as, "the truth that God calls us to himself so decisively that everything we are, everything we do, and everything we have is invested with a special devotion and dynamism lived out as a response to his summons and service."

Think for a moment about the truth that rings in your heart like no other truth you know about life. God doesn't want us to live a weak existence where we allow circumstances to control our decisions. Our calling should push us toward God's best for our lives. There most likely will be struggle, failure, risk, and sorrow involved. But the rewards of such pursuit will far outweigh any trial.

So do you want to be a film director and redeem the world of film? Answer your call. Do you want to be a godly mother and raise your children to love Jesus? Answer your call. Do you want to own your own business and minister to your clients that come through your door? Answer your call. And when you do answer the call, you will be much more inclined to have the stamina to leave this life and know you finished well.

Real Life Strategies:
* Read about great men and women who took risks to fulfill the dream God placed on their hearts.

- Find friends and family who can support you in your calling, so that when you want to give up, others will be cheering you on.

- Pray for God's leading and for sensitivity to know what God has placed in your heart to do.

- Realize perseverance is a must. Do not resign to what you think is second best for you. Never give up. God had something in mind for your hands to do specifically when He created you.

- Beware of any loyalty that competes with your relationship with Christ. Even your "calling" can become an idol.

Real Life Wisdom:

We may retire from our jobs but never from our calling. We may at times be unemployed, but no one ever becomes uncalled. – Os Guinness

Savvy Resources for Additional Study:
The Call: Finding and Fulfilling the Central Purpose of Your Life
By Os Guinness (Word: Nashville, 1998)

The Purpose-Driven Life
By Rick Warren

Scribbling in the Sand: Christ and Creativity
By Michael Card (Downers Grove, Ill: InterVarsity Press, 2002)

PROBLEMS WITH
FAMILY AND FRIENDS

And he said to him, "Son, you are always with me, and all that I have is yours. It was right that we should make merry and be glad, for your brother was dead and is alive again, and was lost and is found."
Luke 15:31-32

32.
HOW DO I PARENT A REBELLIOUS KID?

Real Life Question:

I've tried everything on my son. He just is very strong willed and seems to always choose the opposite of what I tell him. How do you parent a rebellious child?

Every child has a different personality, and some do challenge their parents more than others. What is the proper perspective of discipline as a parent and how can you teach your child to make better choices?

Real Life Case Study:

Shane was only eight years old, but struggling to stay out of the principal's office. It seemed like he was always in trouble at school and at home.

Nancy and Karl were tired and unsure how to get him to behave. Their oldest son, Ian, never challenged them like this. They couldn't figure it out. Had they done something wrong?

"Karl, what are we going to do? Shane is in trouble again at school."

"Well, I just don't know if grounding him one more time is going to do any good. I'm just really embarrassed. Ian just didn't act like this."

"I know, I know. I'm just afraid that we were lax with Shane when he came along because Ian was so easy. I just know I'm running out of energy. What if it is just all our fault and we've messed him up for life? I just really think I don't get him and just feel lost on how to parent. It's really hard to not just feel like a failure."

1. Think about your goals as a Christian parent. What kind of child do you want to raise? Is your end goal for them to be obedient children? Do you want them to go to college? Are you more concerned with outward appearances or the soul of your child?

2. Our children can cause us to be very angry. Read Psalm 4:4; Ephesians 4:26; and James 1:19. Do you feel like you struggle with sinning in your anger? What does loving discipline look like to you?

3. What was your temperament as a child? Were you compliant or more rebellious in nature?

4. Read Joshua 24:15. The reality is we may have two or three rebellious children to raise. How can your household continue to serve the Lord through your role as a parent?

Real Life Lessons:
Parenting can be baffling and confusing at times. The honest

truth is some children are tougher to raise than others. When it comes to raising our children, there are a million things we can worry about—their emotional, spiritual, physical, and social well-being. When we find our child is more inclined to make poor choices and becomes rebellious, the worrying can intensify.

As parents, how our children behave is directly tied to how good of a job we feel we are doing. Guilt often follows us around when we see a child is struggling with rebellion. However, we know that there are examples in the Bible of faithful servants who had unruly children (Samuel); and vice versa, we also have examples of rebellious rulers who had godly children (Hezekiah). Even if we never made a mistake as parents, we really don't have a guarantee that our children will choose wisely. When dealing with a rebellious child, parents need to remember to not be paralyzed with guilt.

There is hope for even the rebellious child. A parent must have both unconditional love and strong control present in the relationship. You may have a very tough kid, and you just have to be a bit tougher to have control. Be alert and one step ahead of them. Make sure you establish clear boundaries and hold the reins in the home. Though it can be easier and tempting, don't give in to your child's bad behavior. When you do this, you give them authority. A child is not capable of handling such freedoms at an early age. Loving control will help save you from having more serious behavioral problems when your child is older.

If you are honest, your rebellious child may push you to your limits, and feel a lot of anger toward them. Anger in itself is not wrong. A lot of parents think they are supposed to always be nice, but the Bible never admonishes us to be "nice" parents. Just as our Heavenly Father shows His wrath, so do we show anger when our children misbehave. We have a right to be angry at sinful acts that our children commit. But we do not have a right to display uncontrolled anger. Godly parental anger can motivate children toward good behavior.

Unconditional love must always be present in the home. This does not mean you do not discipline or correct them when they make wrong choices. Rather, when we love our children in godly ways, we are showing we are concerned for their well-being. Even when a rebellious child messes up horribly, he or she must know that the parent's love is constant, no matter what they do. If a child senses that they are no good or hated, deep resentment can settle in the relationship.

The story of the Prodigal Son is a great example of the hope we must hold out for our children. The father forgave his repentant son and joyfully welcomed him home, even though he was living a sinful life. No child should be cut off from hope, no matter how old they are.

Real Life Strategies:

• Set boundaries in your home starting in the high chair. Respect for authority can be learned when a child is an infant.

• Never, ever give up on your child, and persevere in prayer.

• Have a healthy balance of love and control in the home. Both are necessary for a child to feel secure and safe.

• Make sure you have special time with your child so that they sense that you enjoy their company.

Real Life Wisdom:
There is in repentance this great mystery—that we may fly fastest home on broken wing.—William Sullivan

Savvy Resources for Additional Study:
Bringing Up Boys
By James Dobson

For additional articles on discipline, go to Focus on the Family's Web site: www.fotf.org

Sacred Parenting
By Gary Thomas (Grand Rapids, MI: Zondervan, 2004)

The Mystery of Children: What Our Kids Teach Us about Childlike Faith
By Mike Mason (Colorado Springs, CO: Waterbrook Press, 2001)

Honor your father
and mother,
which is the first
commandment
with promise: that
it may be well with
you and you may live
long on the earth.
And you, fathers, do
not provoke your
children to wrath,
but bring them up
in the training and
admonition of the
Lord.
Ephesians 6:2-4

33.

SHOULD I MAKE MY KIDS GO TO CHURCH WITH ME?

Real Life Question:

I can't seem to get the kids motivated to go. Should I make my kids go to church? I hate it that Sundays feel like war at our house.

Sundays can be nothing more than a drag, a struggle, and big disappointment. Fighting with kids and convincing them they need to go to church, even when they don't feel like it, is a major battle.

Real Life Case Study:

Mandy and Dean have two kids, who have both have become verbal about not wanting to go to church. Dean seems to think they should be able to make their own choices and is afraid of cramming Christianity down their throats. Mandy knows the ill-effects of growing up in a home without God, and she feels it is just fine to apply force.

"Mom, I don't want to go this week. I already know what Bible story we are going to learn and I've heard the same things over and over. I'm just bored with my class," explained Lilly.

"Lilly, first of all, you have to realize that we are your parents and we want what is best for you. You are only ten, and you don't have all the answers."

"Hey, Mom, speaking of church, me and the guys are going to be working really late on a science project Saturday night. I just want to warn you not to wake me up for church," warned Todd, their fifteen-year-old.

"Oh, here we go. More excuses and more resistance for ol' Mom to deal with. Todd, it is great you are so excited about your science project, but nothing is more important than you taking time for worship. End of discussion, you are going."

"Mom, don't you think I'm capable of determining when I should go to church? I can still pray from home and stuff when I get up."

"No, I don't think you're old enough to know what is best. Sorry. I don't want to hear either of you complain about getting up for church."

1. Did you grow up in a home where you were forced to go to church? Did you resent it at the time, but appreciate it later?

2. When do you think a child is old enough to take responsibility for themselves spiritually?

3. Read Proverbs 22:6. Think of children you know who rebelled for a time, then came back to their faith. What brought them back to God?

4. Read Deuteronomy 6:4-9. Do you feel like you are able to bring God into all aspects of your life? Take a moment and think of some ways that where you can better talk with your child as you walk around in your neighborhood, as you lie down at night, as you go about your daily tasks.

Real Life Lessons:

Raising kids to love God is tough. Each phase of life brings new challenges for parents, and teaching a child to love God, no matter what phase of development they are in, is a tough calling. Making God real in every stage of life is our duty. But the church today is competing with all kinds of strong voices in our culture. Kids expect to be entertained all the time. The church has also placed pressure to be a place where there are new bells and whistles each week so that they come back. But what do parents do when their kids don't think it is fun anymore or find they would rather be somewhere else? Remembering a few things about the nature of children can help.

Remember to always set an example for them in regard to your own pursuit of God. As parents, we can put forth a strong effort in being consistent in church attendance, but we also need to take it a step further in putting God first in all areas of life. If your child senses that you go out of guilt or duty yourself, he or she will also be less inclined to go. First and foremost, make sure God is a priority in your own life, not just church attendance. Kids are very smart and discern more about their parents than they often communicate or verbalize. Their eyes are always watching you. Your spiritual life can be a good or bad example to them.

Also remember kids aren't robots that can be programmed to act just how we want. Your child is creatively designed in the image of God, who lives with freedom of choice, just like we have. They have wills, desires, and dreams that are very real to them. They also have their own thoughts and their understanding of God is in progress. Try and get to know them spiritually. Sometimes we forget that there is a lot going on in the hearts and minds of our children, and it is very important to listen well to them and for them to feel that they really have been heard.

If your child is going through a phase where they don't want to go to church, remember your job is only to guide and be an example. You may bear some of the responsibility of their apathy toward church, but it is helpful to remember that you cannot save your child, only God can. Moving toward God, and moving away from God, are all part of your child's spiritual journey. Assure them of God's love always, whether they are rebellious, complacent, or apathetic toward Him.

But parents should not hesitate to strongly encourage their children to go to church. Children need to learn that discipline is a part of life and that we have to make efforts even in our spiritual walk, even when we don't feel like it. God is not a vending machine, or a magic Genie in a bottle. He requires us to sacrifice and suffer sometimes. In reality kids could stand a little boredom and learning how to cope with difficulties.

There will come a day when parents have to let their children make their own choices in regard to their spiritual life. While they are under your covering and at home, you do have a say—a big say—with what they do on Sunday. But as they get older, a healthy parent-child relationship changes and more freedoms are given. As they mature, questions about God will only increase, and most likely, they will be first to initiate the leaving process. This prepares them for adulthood. Matthew 4:22 says that when Jesus called James and John, immediately they left the boat *and their father* to follow Him. To let go will be one of the hardest phases of parenting, but if you have made God real in the home throughout the tough, growing years, a few failures to get them in the pew on Sundays will be insignificant. To release them to God is a part of the parenting process, which allows them to ultimately do great things for His kingdom.

Real Life Strategies:

● If your child is fighting your requirement to go to church, think about your own church attendance. What does it communicate to them?

● Realize if your child does win on one Sunday and stays home to sleep in, that you did not lose the war. God is still at work in the heart of your child.

● You cannot save them; only God can.

● Be faithful to pray daily for your child's spiritual walk with God.

Real Life Wisdom:

Children today are tyrants. They contradict their parents, gobble their food, and tyrannize their teachers. —Socrates (470-399 BC)

The way up is the way down, the way forward is the way back. — T.S. Eliot

Savvy Resources for Additional Study:
Sacred Parenting
By Gary Thomas (Grand Rapids: Zondervan, 2004)

Visit Focus on the Family's Web site for various parenting articles
www.fotf.org

Counsel in the
heart of man is
like deep water,
but a man of
understanding
will draw it out.
Proverbs 20:5

34.
HOW SHOULD A WIFE COPE WITH A PASSIVE HUSBAND?

Real Life Question:

My husband is a godly man, but has not shown an interest in leading our home spiritually.

Real Life Case Study:

Sue and Paul were instantly attracted to each other when they met at Bible college years ago. They had so much in common and knew God had brought them together. But as the years went by, Sue grew continually disheartened by Paul's spiritual passivity. She felt like she was all alone in raising her boys to love and respect God.

Sue grew up in a home where her father led their home spiritually. He was very verbal about his faith and led the family in devotions and prayer. Naturally Sue expected this is what would be demonstrated in their home. When their two boys came along, Sue's aggravation with Paul intensified.

"Paul, I need you to start leading our boys spiritually. I feel all alone here, and I'm asking for your help. The fact that you don't go to church every Sunday is a problem for me."

"Sue, you aren't my spiritual compass, God is. Okay, so I don't go every Sunday. I don't think God loves me any less."

"No, you are right. He doesn't love you any less, but I'm concerned that this communicates church is not important to the boys. Can you just not think about yourself on this one, and see it from the eyes of the boys? I want them to know how to lead their families spiritually one day, and I don't think you are modeling that for them."

"Hey, they know I love God. You don't know all that we talk about."

"Well, these are tough years for the boys, and I'm just afraid you aren't overt enough about your spiritual life. ... I'm scared for them."

Paul rolls his eyes and walks out.

1. Do you feel like Sue's challenge to Paul was fair? What is your response in dealing with a spiritually passive husband?

2. If you are struggling with spiritual passivity in your home, think about how you can draw your husband closer to God. What outlets can you encourage him to pursue without nagging?

3. What does your prayer life look like for your husband? Make a stronger commitment to pray for him in specific ways. List some areas in his life that you can pray about that you have neglected.

4. Read Ephesians 5:23-31. Record any new insights you have found that can be of help to you at this time.

Real Life Lessons:

Often it is the women who wear the spiritual pants in the home. Our churches today have more women in attendance than men. Most men would admit that their wives have contributed more to the spiritual temperament of their home than they have. How can women help to change this fact?

In Sue's case, she grew up in a Christian home where her father took the spiritual lead. She knew this was God's design and expected the same of Paul. Though we do not know Paul's upbringing from the scenario, reflecting on your husband's past may be helpful, giving you insight in how to support him spiritually. Paul's mom could have been the spiritual leader in their home. It may be quite natural for him to allow Sue to take on that responsibility, though he knows as a father he has a responsibility as well. Or, he could have parents that were not Christians at all, having few examples of what spiritual leadership looks like in a home.

If you are a wife who struggles with a passive husband, think for a moment about things in his life that may be hindering his relationship with God. Prayer is an important part of being a godly wife. Sometimes God does call us to confront the situation and share honestly with our husband, and sometimes we are called to be longsuffering in prayer. Be always quick to listen and slow to speak, especially if you are unsure about what more to do. Remember, ultimately God is the head of our household and the spiritual father to your children when your husband is not fulfilling that role properly.

In this difficult situation, prayer cannot be overemphasized. Pray, pray, pray. Make a commitment to pray specifically for your husband, expecting nothing in return from him. Focus on all aspects of his life, not just his passive spiritual leadership. His inability or lack of desire to lead may be tied to other parts of his life. God can reveal to us many things that we cannot know in our own conventional wisdom when we pray and ask for counsel. There could be other areas of his life that God needs to work on first that is hindering him from taking up his responsibility to lead spiritually. Pray for greater understanding. Maybe your husband is struggling with his work, his faith, his self-image, his image of God, or his level of confidence. Ask God to show you how to prayerfully support all areas of his life. You may find it is another area that is paralyzing him from growth in this area.

Then think about your own tendencies. Ask God to reveal to you any ways that you might be hindering your husband's innate desire to lead. Do you think he feels respected by you? Are you taking too much control over the spiritual environment of your home? In what ways might you be enabling bad behavior?

Mutual respect is important when a husband and wife are struggling with an issue. If a husband does not feel respected, he can retreat further from his wife and from God. If a wife is naturally good at leading spiritually, she can come across as self-righteous and too independent. Be mindful of your posture when you communicate with your spouse and ask your husband to lead spiritually. God may also want to do a work in you so that there is room for your husband to change.

Be encouraged and rejoice in the progress you see, no matter how small. Be grateful that your husband does love God and that nothing is impossible with God.

Real Life Strategies:

• Be willing to give up control of your husband's spiritual life. It is ultimately God's responsibility.

• Trust that God knows the heart of your husband better than you and He can move in unexpected ways.

• Recall the times when your husband has shown initiative spiritually and thank him for such times.

• Never give up on prayer. Many of life's problems are solved through a simple and strong commitment to prayer.

Real Life Wisdom:

Praying for your husband will be an act of unselfish, unconditional love and sacrifice on your part. You must be willing to make this commitment knowing it is quite possible—even highly probably—that he will never pray for you in the same way. ... Regardless, whether he does or doesn't is not your concern, it's God's. –Stormie Omartian

Savvy Resources for Additional Study:
The Power of a Praying Wife
By Stormie Omartian (Eugene, OR: Harvest House, 1997)

Love and Respect
By Emerson Eggerichs (Nashville: Integrity, 2006)

Love suffers long and is kind; love does not envy; love does not parade itself, is not puffed up; does not behave rudely, does not seek its own, is not provoked, thinks no evil; does not rejoice in iniquity, but rejoices in the truth; bears all things, believes all things, hopes all things, endures all things. Love never fails.

I Corinthians 13:4-7

35.
WHEN IS IT ENOUGH IN A MARRIAGE?

Real Life Question:

Some say we have tried hard as any couple to stay together. When is it time to just call it quits in marriage?

Marriage can be the most rewarding relationship or the most wearisome. Sometimes it feels like enduring any more hardship would be impossible. What does God require us to do when it comes to holding our marriages together?

Real Life Case Study:

Jason and Sarah have struggled for several years to just hang on. Both have been in counseling and are Christians. Things go well for a time, but then they often find themselves right where they started.

Early in their marriage, Sarah felt neglected, alone, and afraid. Looking back, she thinks they may have married too young. After a few years into their marriage, she had an affair. She confessed her sin to God and to Jason. As expected, Jason took it hard and started to have doubts of his own worth. This took its toll on Sarah emotionally, as she felt like she could never make it up to Jason.

Jason had a drinking problem ever since Sarah knew him. She didn't think he was an alcoholic, but was aware that sometimes he couldn't seem to stop. As they continued on in their marriage, the problem grew worse and Sarah did not know how to help him. She just knew she didn't respect him.

Both Jason and Sarah come from divorced homes and didn't have strong role models as to what a Christian home should look like. There were some red flags raised in their premarital counseling, but they just wanted to move away from home and get married. They went into their relationship vowing to not be like their parents and stay committed, not matter what. Yet, neither of them would say they were happy in their relationship.

After a heated argument, Sarah determined it was time to end the pain they were causing each other. She decided to file for divorce.

1. In knowing what you know about Sarah and Jason, do you think they have biblical grounds for divorce? Why or why not?

2. When have you wanted to give up on your marriage?

3. Take time to read the book of Hosea. God called Hosea to marry a prostitute. Think about God's love for His bride, the Church, and his willingness to persevere. How does this affect your view of divorce?

4. What do you think is the purpose of marriage from God's perspective? How does it differ from the world's view of marriage?

5. Why do you think divorce is so pervasive in Christian marriages today?

Real Life Lessons:

Think about a wedding day. Family and friends gather to celebrate love and future hope. The church is buzzing with excitement as everyone takes their place to witness the wedding vows. The bride is stunningly beautiful in her gown, waiting for the sanctuary doors to open, marking the beginning of her new life. Her dream of being a wife has come true. The groom stands at the front of the church, eager to take on the responsibility of being a husband and anticipates his new job will bring them a good, stable start. They both love God and each other. But is it enough?

Our culture has made marriage to mean something different than what God intended. A wrong view of marriage can cause Christian couples to be at a greater risk of giving up. If you view marriage as the road to happiness, you either have experienced severe disappointment, or soon will.

When we decide that marriage is for us and not remaining single, we then are called to an entirely new selfless kind of living. In his book *Sacred Marriage*, Gary Thomas points out that the real purpose of marriage is not our happiness, but rather our holiness. This doesn't mean God is opposed to happiness, but seeing holiness as the end goal puts a different spin on the bond of marriage. When the focus is on temporal happiness, most find that any spouse will not be able to live up to the expectations imposed by this view, and the tendency is to bail out.

Any man or woman entering marriage brings with them their sin to the relationship. With God's help they will seek to put one another first, but each person will fail in this from time to time. Some of us have asked too much of our spouse and too much of marriage. Our expectations are to find fulfillment, but we were never designed to find fulfillment in anyone except God.

Marriage doesn't have to lead to misery and despair in our quest for holiness, but it has to be about much more than our own happiness. The more you love God, the better spouse you will naturally be.

When things feel unbearable in your marriage, remember God may be using your spouse to refine you more into His image. God says that He hates divorce (Malachi 2:16), though He made provision for it. There are circumstances when divorce is necessary.

You may feel like your needs are not being met in your marriage and have looked to other means for fulfillment. Perhaps you are dealing with infidelity and very deep sin issues. Most of your friends might even be telling you it is time to say, "enough is enough," and move on. But even infidelity doesn't have to destroy or end your marriage.

Marriage can bring us a great deal of fulfillment and contentment. But there are times in the Christian life when we are called to lay aside our happiness and dutifully fulfill our Christian obligation. If we as Christians are ambassadors of Christ and are proclaiming His Gospel, then we should strive to persevere in our marriage as we proclaim His ministry of reconciliation.

Struggling is a part of any relationship, and we should expect it and offer it up to God to mold us more into His likeness. Happiness will naturally come when we put God first, not ourselves. To make marriage work, we have to radically be committed to discipleship. If we view marriage as a holy relationship that will bring us purposefully toward God, we will be willing to fight out even the toughest situations. Christ is our example in the way of love as He shows us His unwavering commitment to His Bride, the church. Draw from Christ's example, not our culture, which often tells us to give up too soon.

Real Life Strategies:

• The deepest struggles we have in life will be lived out in the context of marriage.

• Marriage helps us to be better servants.

• Marriage allows ourselves to see the depth of our sin and our profound need for God.

• Just because God made provision for divorce doesn't mean you have to use that provision.

Real Life Wisdom:

If you want to be free to serve Jesus, there's no question—stay single. Marriage takes a lot of time. But if you want to become more like Jesus, I can't imagine any better thing to do than to get married.
—Gary Thomas

Savvy Resources for Additional Study:
Sacred Marriage
By Gary Thomas (Grand Rapids, MI: Zondervan, 2001)
The Mystery of Marriage By Mike Mason

Then the king instructed Ashpenaz, the master of his eunuchs, to bring some of the children of Israel and some of the king's descendants and some of the nobles, young men in whom there was no blemish, but good-looking, gifted in all wisdom, possessing knowledge and quick to understand, who had ability to serve in the king's palace, and whom they might teach the language and literature of the Chaldeans.

Daniel 1:3-4

36.

HOW SHOULD I DECIDE ABOUT EDUCATION FOR MY KIDS?

Real Life Question:

How do I know if I should send our kids to public or private schools, or should we opt for home schooling?

Education is an important part of a child's life, and sometimes there are pros and cons for each option. What should parents really know about education?

Real Life Case Study:

Scenario #1: Katy loved her school and reached seventh grade never feeling out of place for being a Christian, until her science teacher refused to teach the view of Creation. Katy knew that evolution was not the only credible view, even in the science world. So she decided to write a paper on creationism, instead of evolution. Her teacher gave her an "F," because she ignored the assignment rules. Katy's parents knew this was her choice and they were proud of her ability to stand up for truth. Katy's parents believe strongly that their children are called to be in the public schools to make a difference.

Scenario #2: The Johnstons noticed that Greg was acting rather distant and didn't seem to care about some of his friends anymore. Recently he had been hanging with a new group of kids, who were usually in trouble and looked rough. Pam and Marty knew that kids go through phases and thought that would try and ride this out and see if Greg's behavior changed much more.

One day Pam was looking for Greg's jacket to wash, and found some drugs in his pocket. That evening they sat down and talked. Greg was very emotional and confessed he needed help. Pam and Marty decided the best thing for their son was to put him in a Christian school. Through prayer and counseling, they made the move quickly.

Scenario #3: Tim and Cheryl were finding themselves to already be approaching the school years for Nicole. She was very bright and eager to learn. They considered public and private schools for a couple of years and Cheryl visited the classrooms to have a feel for the environment. She was excited to find that a new charter school would be opened by the time Nicole was ready for school.

As she experienced various classrooms, Cheryl felt that a classroom could not provide the moral teaching she wanted Nicole to learn. Being a teacher herself, she never thought she would be one to consider home schooling, but after thoroughly exploring the options, it made sense for their family. She knew that the one-on-one teaching would be most productive and really liked the fact that both she and Tim would have full control over the curriculum.

1. What kind of education do you want for your children?

2. Think about your own elementary education. What was good or bad about it?

3. Read Proverbs 1:2-5; 8:12-16 in light of the education process. How can we teach our children that wisdom is more important than just knowledge?

4. How can parents integrate faith and learning more effectively?

Real Life Lessons:

Education today offers families more options to consider than before. For Christians, public, private, or home school education are viable options. It is important to realize that there is no one right answer. There are some basic concepts about education that can be of help as you plan for the best education opportunity available for your children.

As parents, no matter what mode of education you choose, you must be involved. Parents exert a very positive influence on their child's achievements in school. The Christian worldview must be talked about as you talk about academic disciplines. Our view of God should not be something just for Sunday school. How we view the sciences and approach other disciplines like English and

History are all informed by our Christian worldview. Be involved and teach your children to integrate faith and learning.

Consider also the goals you should have for your child's education. What kind of person do you want them to be when they grow up? What subjects are most important for their life skills and future goals? It is important to have a basic philosophy of education when making your education choices. Education should answer: Who are we as humans? What is our purpose in life? How can we equip ourselves for the tasks of life?

Most of us have heard about the decline in education. This isn't necessarily due to bad teachers or poor teaching and a lack of funding. Unfortunately many schools deny the benefits of believing in absolute truth and morality. Part of the forgotten task of education is to teach children to grow up and be good citizens that contribute to society.

Saint Augustine asked this question in his *Solilquies*: "What do you want to know?" He replied, "God and the soul, nothing else!" He argued that there were three branches of philosophy: natural philosophy, where God is the source of all of life; rational philosophy, where God is the source of all knowledge and truth; and moral philosophy, in which He is the source of all that is good. From his own struggles, Augustine knew that the heart, soul, and mind were all connected and to separate them only causes disorder and a fractured view of the world. Integrating God was essential for Augustine, and he ultimately knew students needed to know that God held absolute authority. To not know this core belief only leads to despair.

You may find as parents God is calling you to help reform public education and to place your children in public schools. Or, you may find that the best way for you to give your child a fully developed Christian worldview is to opt for a private school education. Still after weighing the pros of cons of these two options, you are convinced home schooling is best. Whatever you choose, make sure you are committed to being involved in the moral development of your child, emphasizing to them that Christianity is the great defender of reason, essential to all of life and education.

Real Life Strategies:

* Remember education is not just about intelligence. It involves the whole person that is in pursuit of truth—which is God.

* Before making a decision about schooling, seek to know your child well and how he or she learns best.

* Take responsibility in keeping your child engaged and interested in their education.

* Did you know Winston Churchill, Charles Dickens, Florence Nightingale, and Benjamin Franklin were all home schooled?

* Do not look down on your other Christian friends who have consciously made a different choice than yours.

Real Life Wisdom:
Christ is the teacher within us. –St. Augustine

Savvy Resources for Additional Study:
On Christian Teaching
By Saint Augustine (Oxford University Press

Building the Christian Academy
By Arthur F. Holms (Grand Rapids, MI: Wm. B. Eerdmans
Publishing Co., 2001)

*Philosophy and Education: An Introduction in Christian
Perspective*
By George R. Knight (Berrien Springs, MI: Andrews
University Press, 1998)

For I say, through the grace given to me, to everyone who is among you, not to think of himself more highly than he ought to think, but to think soberly, as God has dealt to each one a measure of faith.

Romans 12:3

37.
CAN I BE FRIENDS WITH SOMEONE WHO IS GAY?

Real Life Question:

How can I befriend a homosexual without condoning that lifestyle? I'm just not even sure I can relate to such a problem and really don't know what to say.

Homosexuality is a growing problem in society, and the church often feels ill-equipped in reaching out. Most churches are unsure how to evangelize this community. What is our moral responsibility as Christians?

Real Life Case Study:

Patty hadn't been back to her hometown in over ten years. She was looking forward to seeing her friends from grade school and high school at her class reunion.

After arriving, she was amazed at how many friends were exactly the same as she remembered them to be. She also was surprised at some of her friends that she did not even recognize, in particular, Stephen.

"Patty, I have a surprise. Close your eyes. You aren't going to believe who is here!" shrieked Nancy.

Patty followed her quickly, trying to remember those she lost touch with. She opened her eyes, and stood a bit stunned. She saw a man in a turquoise velvet coat with very expensive looking shoes. He had a kind smile, but looked like no one she remembered. Then she looked into the man's eyes and knew exactly who it was.

"Stephen Squires! I can't believe it! How are you?" she squealed as she hugged him.

Stephen was one of the smart boys in her class and always did the right thing. He was conservative, so she always felt safe hanging out with him. Patty and Stephen and a group of friends would all go roller skating on Fridays. Patty recalled having a slight crush on him, and she felt comfortable around him, unlike some of the other boys in her class.

"Well, you look the same, Patty. I would have recognized you anywhere. Amazing, but seems time stood still for you."

"Nice of you to say, Stephen. What happened to you in high school? I lost track of you."

"I actually had some really rough years. My parents shipped me off to boarding school after I got kicked out of West High. I actually started doing drugs right after we graduated and just couldn't kick it for a long time.... I guess it was around that time I realized I was gay."

Patty suspected it right away from his appearance. He was painfully thin, very manicured, and bragged about his designer lifestyle and his $500 boots.

"I'm glad to see old friends, Patty. I just broke up with my partner, and we were not in agreement about kids. I wanted them, and he didn't. He would have been a terrible parent, anyway. He is a workaholic ... anyway my life has been a sort of a mess of late."

Patty talked to Stephen for several hours and the reminisced like seventh grade was yesterday. He knew she was a Christian, but she was afraid to talk about her faith for fear he would think she hated him.

1. Do you know someone who is struggling with homosexuality? What is your relationship like?

2. Read I Corinthians 9:6-11. Think for a moment how you view the sin of homosexuality. Do you find yourself thinking this sin is greater than others?

3. What are some of the harmful consequences that can hurt those caught up in this lifestyle? Physically? Emotionally? Spiritually?

Real Life Lessons:

Among Christians, homosexuals often feel like lepers. The church at large has not done a good job in addressing this complex issue, nor have we welcomed the homosexual into the body of Christ, giving them answers about their struggles.

Think about how many people you know in your church who are struggling with a sin issue, yet most likely they are not chastised like a homosexual would be at your church. What can we do to establish relationships with the gay community? If we do not, how will they ever know God's unconditional love for them as well as His truth that could restore their lives?

First, it helps to understand the mind of the homosexual. Most have had trauma of some kind in their family relationships. Some had a domineering mother or a passive father. Even worse, some have been victims of sexual abuse. There is a reason for their attraction to the same sex, which is usually due to dysfunctional views of themselves.

Many gay people think because they felt attraction for the opposite sex as a child that they're gay. Thoughts like these are normal and do not mean someone has to turn to that lifestyle. This is a lie that the gay subculture has engrained in them, as most want to belong somewhere, succumb to the pressure, and join the *family*.

In most cases, homosexuals are outcasts of the family and are looking for acceptance. The last place they expect to find it is in the church, tragically. They soon are taken care of by the gay community and reeled into the drug culture and often multiple partners. As same sex relationships come and go, a gay person can begin to move more and more inward, toward self. Flamboyant dress is common for men. Any extreme experience should just be taken in stride as a friend.

Homosexuality is something that causes a level of self-absorption and is a self-destructive lifestyle because it goes against God's created order. As you get to know a gay friend better, you will see the despair and empty relationships that are really their reality. When you get to that point and your friend is more vulnerable with you, it will be natural to talk about a better life, a life that leads to relationship blessing, not despair.

Try and invite your homosexual friend to your own family events. Let them see strong, fulfilling marriages and experience family that really cares for each other. He or she can be drawn in by the testimony of your family's relationships.

Real Life Strategies:

- Before you can really share God's best for them, you have to earn the right to speak into their life. Relationship is essential.

- Treat them like you would any other friend and remind yourself that all of us have fallen into sin.

- Establish good, honest, open communication. You don't have to compromise your beliefs. Agree to disagree in hopes of leaving the door open for conversations about what God thinks about homosexuality.

- Be confident that truth does matter and that the Christian worldview can free a person from being in bondage to the gay lifestyle.

- Homosexuals have often been told they cannot change. Encourage them that freedom can be found through a new life in Christ.

Real Life Wisdom:

God is infinitely just. I don't believe He would speak of homosexuality in the Scriptures as an abominable sin and list it among the most despicable of human behaviors if men and women bore no responsibility for engaging in it (see 1 Corinthians 6:9-10). That is not how He does business. —Dr. James Dobson

Savvy Resources for Additional Study:

Exodus International Ministries offers support to those wishing to overcome the gay lifestyle. You can find local counselors in your area that can be of help to family and friends. www.exodus-international.org

Homosexuality 101: Where Does It Come From, Is Change Possible, and How Should Christians Respond?
by Julie Harren

When Homosexuality Hits Home: What to do When a Loved One Says They're Gay
by Joe Dallas (Harvest House Publishers)

> For since the creation of the world His invisible attributes are clearly seen, being understood by the things that are made, even His eternal power and Godhead, so that they are without excuse.
>
> **Romans 1:20**

38.

HOW CAN I TALK TO MY FRIENDS ABOUT SPIRITUALITY?

Real Life Question:

My friends know that I am a Christian, but I wish I knew how to bring up issues about spirituality in a non-threatening manner. I don't ever want to come across as better than they are, and I'm not sure how to naturally make it a part of conversation.

When sharing our faith with someone, often there is a need to do some pre-evangelism before sharing specifics about Christianity. Getting others to acknowledge that the human race was created as spiritual beings is a part of the process.

Real Life Case Study:

Richard belonged to a cycling club. His friend Sam from church also was a part of the group. Both had met some great friends, and enjoyed the workout. Tragically, one of the cyclists had a freak accident and died just as they started to get to know him. After the funeral, Richard and Sam sat in the parking lot talking it over.

"Richard, it is hard to believe Steve isn't going to be with us every Saturday anymore."

"Yeah. I'm still in shock. I wasn't far behind him when his bike swerved out of control. I wish I could have done something . . .I just looked back and ..." Sam broke down and sobbed.

"Sam, you were a great friend and we were just getting to know him. You know, he mentioned he used to go to church but had wandered away, just got tired of hypocrisy that he saw. I never got around to asking him if he considered himself to be a Christian, but we did talk about spiritual things sometimes."

"You know, before the funeral, a couple days ago, I decided to call his wife to see how she was doing. She said she felt so lost and empty and was mad that people were saying Steve was in a better place. She thinks this is it, that there is no eternal life for anyone. Paula said she has no need for any god or superstitious crutch."

"I wish I would have taken more opportunities to talk to Steve so I could be more sure about his faith. We were getting close to talking about the stuff that matters in life. If I had, maybe Paula would realize we are all just looking for spiritual fulfillment. I don't know if Steve and Paula shared the same beliefs or not. Right now, she doesn't even acknowledge her need to worship something outside of herself."

"Well, Richard, we may have a lot of opportunities to help her. She is a widow now. I think there are ways we can talk about spirituality, especially when we are all faced with our mortality."

1. Most people acknowledge a spiritual dimension that we need to nourish, and that there is a bigger force than

themselves holding the universe together. Have you found this to be true?

2. Read Romans 1:18-25.What are some ways you can think of to bring up spiritual matters in everyday conversations?

3. Think about the spiritual needs you see in those around you. What are some common ways in which everyone pursues spirituality?

4. How does unexpected trauma open doors to explore spirituality?

Real Life Lessons:

When talking with others about spirituality, it probably won't take long to recognize if someone believes in a supernatural dimension or not. If they do not, they would adhere to a *closed system*, which makes no room for God. Such a worldview would be called naturalism. Naturalism has been a popular force in culture and has even crept into our Christian spirituality.

Evolution is based on naturalism—we are at the mercy of nature. The world came about through natural forces of the universe. Life is a random act and finding purpose for life is very difficult in a closed system.

If we are honest with ourselves, we do sense an innate desire to worship and to seek out what is right and good. This natural inclination witnesses to our spirituality. Whether someone acknowledges it or not, we were all created with the inclination to worship. If you think about it, you can see evidence that everyone does worship something. People can worship God, false gods, a job, a spouse, money, or even themselves. If we do not worship the One True God, our souls will look to another source to fulfill the void. We cannot avoid worshipping something.

One way to bring up spirituality with a non-Christian is to talk about his or her dreams and desires. Usually these are connected to our spiritual dimension, as we all have the need to feel like life is more than just what we can see in the natural. Find out if your friend is living a life that matters to them. Chances are, they will quickly tell you they are not fulfilled and aren't sure what they are looking for, but know inherently that they have not found it. Having honest conversations about the meaning of life can quickly move toward an acknowledgment of another world beyond what we know. And if our spiritual dimension is not nurtured by God Himself, we will not find the contentment we were created to have in this life.

The nonbeliever may talk about having a faith or feeling like faith is important, but most likely cannot articulate the object of his or her faith, so they turn inward. For the Christian our faith has an Object, who is God and turns us outward.

Sometimes we do come across as threatening or as a Bible thumper because we have not met our friend on the right plane of commonality. We know God's Word is powerful and active, but it may not sound relevant to someone who doesn't believe it to be true. Forget about quoting all the right verses and begin to listen to the heart and soul of the friends around you, and you may be amazed at all the opportunities that open up to talk about spirituality in very natural, unassuming ways. Romans 1:20 tells us the evidence of God is known to all and that we really are without excuse. Some may deny this, but most just need the prodding of a good friend to share their own spiritual journey.

Real Life Strategies:

● Start your conversation about spirituality where it feels natural.

● Have confidence that God is seeking the person you are talking to and has already had impact on their lives that they might not consciously realize. Take comfort in the seeds already planted.

● Don't be afraid to confidently share the fact that a Christian worldview, when tested, actually works.

● Think about the spiritual needs God has met in your life this week and share them with your friend.

Real Life Wisdom:

Whenever men say they are looking for greater reality, we must show them at once the reality of true Christianity . . .

The optimistic jump is a necessity because man is still created in the image of God, whatever he may say about himself, and as such he cannot go on living in meaninglessness. –Francis Schaeffer

Savvy Resources for Additional Study:
True Spirituality
By Francis Schaeffer (Wheaton, Ill: Tyndale, 1971)

The Francis Schaeffer Trilogy: The Three Essential Books in One Volume
By Francis Schaeffer (Wheaton, Ill: Crossway Books, 1990)

Moreover, brethren, we make known to you the grace of God bestowed on the churches of Macedonia: that in a great trial of affliction the abundance of their joy and their deep poverty abounded in the riches of their liberality.

2 Corinthians 8:1-2

39.
HOW CAN I BE GENEROUS WITH MONEY WHILE RAISING A FAMILY?

Real Life Question:

How can we be generous givers when money is really tight? My family has so many different needs that come up, and I don't know what should be a priority.

Most of us know what it is like to live on a tight budget. Perhaps you are a single mom without financial support from others. Or maybe your company has been downsized and you find yourself unemployed. There are distressing times in our lives when it is tempting to forget our biblical mandate to give of our financial resources generously.

Real Life Case Study:

Creekside Community Church is starting up their annual stewardship campaign. The pastor is asking for sacrificial giving as they launch their new building campaign to make room for more children on Sunday morning. Greg dreads the newsletters and announcements that flood his mailbox each year around this time.

"I give my ten percent, and I even serve as a youth sponsor... What more do they want from me? As it is, I have no extra time or money. How can I possibly give any more? If I were rich, I'd pay for the whole new wing, but I'm not a millionaire like some in our church."

Greg receives the newsletter announcing the sermon series, *Money Matters*. He begins to wonder if he should change churches. He feels it is wrong for the church to ask him to be any more generous.

Maybe you can relate to Greg's frustrations. At the end of the day, you too may feel you have tapped out all your resources— mentally, emotionally, and financially. There seems to be nothing left over for even yourself.

One of the hardest battles the Christian has to face in the twenty-first century is *selfism*. Our culture tells us that we must put ourselves first in order to find fulfillment, but this is an anti-Christian sentiment. The Macedonians are examples to us today, who live in the most prosperous times, of what generosity looks like. They did not wait to be rich before they were generous. They gave when it hurt because they knew their priority was first to God. The Old Testament standard was to give God the first ten percent. But the New Testament requires even more, to give generously. 2 Corinthians 8:7 says, "Each man should give what he has decided in his heart to give, not reluctantly or under compulsion, for God loves a cheerful giver."

So how do we give when money is tight? Generously, not sparingly or begrudgingly. We don't have to wait until we win the lottery to give to God and others that are in need. God doesn't expect us to meet every financial need that our church or someone shares with us, but we need to be prayerful in how we are being called to give in our own life context.

1. Read 2 Corinthians 8:1-15. How does the testimony of the Macedonian churches challenge you?

2. Think about someone you know who is a generous person. What are some of their general attitudes about life that you admire?

3. Do you find yourself relating more to Greg, the disgruntled church member, or the generous Macedonian Christians? On a scale of 1-10, rate yourself on how well you are doing with living generously.

4. Besides money, in what other ways can we live generously toward others?

Real Life Lessons:

To give sacrificially can be counterintuitive. Most of us spend all that we earn. Our culture is one that is entrenched in consumerism, and because we work hard, we begin to believe we have earned the right to do as we please with *our* money and time. But for Christians we know that all of what we have is from God—time and money. We are only stewards of the resources He gives us. He has entrusted us to determine what to do with all of our resources.

217

Paul gives us a great challenge on living generously in 2 Corinthians 8. The Macedonian Christians understood the blessing of generous giving. Out of their most severe trials and poverty, they were known for their generosity. The Apostle Paul tells us that they gave beyond their ability, giving themselves first to the Lord. Jesus commended the widow who gave out of her poverty, so we know He takes notice of those who give sacrificially.

The reality is, the more grateful we are, the more inclined we are to live generously. Because we live in an instant-gratification world, we often expect to have everything we want. If we don't have all that our neighbor has, we feel like God isn't blessing us. We have become a generation of consumer Christians. We expect the church to meet our needs, while we sit and take our posture of feasting on all we can get from God. Because the stresses of life and our financial obligations tug and pull at us all week, we view church to be the one place where we don't have to meet any requirements. Though the cultural message screams, "you deserve it all," resist this narcissistic voice and don't let it win over God's call to live out your life with a giving heart. One simple discipline that can help you move toward living generously is to start with acknowledging what God has done for you on a daily basis. Offer a heart of gratitude to God. You may be surprised how much you really do have to give when you take time to recall the generosity of God that is evident around your own life.

Real Life Strategies:
- Don't wait until you're rich to be a generous person.

- Eliminate something from your schedule that will allow you to give time to someone who might need your help.

- No matter what your life situation is right now, take time to be grateful for what God has given to you.

- Resist the voice within that says, "I should come first."

Real Life Wisdom:

As we give away our lives in service—as we lose our lives in order to save them—we discover the true meaning of our lives in the midst of fellowship and community.–Chuck Colson

We make a living by what we get, but we make a life by what we give. –Winston Churchill

Savvy Resources for Additional Study:

Money was a topic that Jesus addressed consistently throughout His ministry. Read the parable of the Rich Young Ruler found in Luke 18:18-27.

You may also want to search for all the passages where Jesus makes a point to talk about money, wealth, and giving.

The Good Life
By Charles Colson (Tyndale, 2005)

April Witt, "Acquiring Minds: Inside America's All-Consuming Passion," Washington Post, December 14, 2003, W14, http://www.washingtonpost.com/wp-dyn/articles/A53732-2003Dec10.html.

I beseech you therefore, brethren, by the mercies of God, that you present your bodies a living sacrifice, holy, acceptable to God, *which is* your reasonable service. And do not be conformed to this world, but be transformed by the renewing of your mind, that you may prove what is that good and acceptable and perfect will of God.

Romans 12:1-2

40. CAN I REALLY LIVE OUT SEXUAL MORALITY?

Real Life Question:

Is it even realistic in this day and age to not have sex outside of marriage? I know what the Bible says, but I just don't see Christians are even able to abstain any better.

Sex is a big idol in our culture. It is the topic of most television sitcoms, and suggestive ads are plastered on billboards and magazines everywhere. Temptations are all around us, but are Christians openly talking about how to resist?

Real Life Case Study:

Kate knew when she made the decision she would live to regret it. Kate met John at church and didn't think she would ever meet a Christian guy that she was actually attracted to. Soon after meeting, they both realized there was a strong attraction to one another.

Soon they began dating and spent most weekends together. John told her that he was struggling with going too far, and wondered if they should try and do some more group dating. Kate confessed her struggle as well, and thought they should talk opening about what they believed about sex.

"Well, I was raised believing sex was for marriage, John, but I'm at a place in my life where I'm not sure. I mean, I really love you, and isn't that what really matters?" shared Kate.

"Well, my folks don't care what I do. I know the Bible said it is for marriage, but I sort of wonder if that standard is even realistic. I mean I just don't know any guy who waits anymore."

"So what should we do?" Kate said with apprehension.

"I think we should listen to our hearts. Seem like the most honest thing. I mean think about food for a minute. Yes, its purpose is for nourishment, but there are many times in we see in the Bible it was for pleasure and celebration. I think sex is like that too. It's not just for procreation, it's also for pleasure."

1. Think about your friends and family who are Christians. Do you feel like Christians in general have a well developed understanding of what they believe about sex?

2. Do you feel like you have made mistakes when it comes to your own sexual ethics? If so, what have you learned about yourself and God's view of sex?

3. How do you try to avoid falling into sexual sin?

4. Read Genesis 1-2. What can we learn about God's idea for sex in what we read about Adam and Eve?

221

Real Life Lessons:

So what do Christians really believe about sex? Most would instinctively know that God has ordained sex for marriage, but it seems few are able to live by what they believe to be true. Unfortunately Christians haven't dialogued enough about sexuality to be able to create a helpful, sound sexual ethic that works out practically in life.

First we have to remember that our bodies are good and holy. Sexuality is not something dirty or sinful. We have to embrace this aspect of our humanity in order to understand what God has to say about it. The body is the temple of the Holy Spirit and we are to see our bodies as a sacred part of God's creation.

Christians often do not realize how culture impacts their beliefs. Just take a moment and think about what the media tells us about sex. It is no longer thought of just in the context of a family or around procreation. Sex is all about entertainment. Such thoughts have shaped our thinking, and if we are not careful we find, dangerously, that we are buying into this ideology. But this is not real sex, it is counterfeit. Two unmarried people who engage in the act do not experience the relational blessing and oneness that only marriage can provide.

In God's economy, sex was never meant to be something to pass the time away or as an act of recreation. It is a sacred act designed for a husband and a wife. When we go against God's laws, there is usually despair and hurtful consequences. God did not make this rule to kill our fun, but rather to protect us because He knows how intimate an act that it really is.

Part of the reason that sex has become the modern god of the twenty-first century is because there is no other act that imitates transcendence like sex. When a man and woman become intimate in this way, they physically become one. This mirrors the Trinity, and even what Jesus prayed for His disciples, that we would be One with our Heavenly Father. Sex touches us spiritually, but many people deny the spiritual dimension.

For Christians to be able to say no to premarital sex or to infidelity there have to be strong convictions as to why it really is harmful. You have to know why you believe what you believe to be able to live it out. Our moral beliefs shouldn't be just theories, but ones that hold up in real life.

Most often when we succumb to temptation, we are trying to fill a spiritual void in our lives, and having someone tangibly there can be a temporarily satisfying substitute for God.

The church could do better at providing sexual ethics 101 for unmarried couples and even for married couples. We know what Jesus said, but aren't convinced if it is for us today. We might not come out and say that, but our actions would prove otherwise.

Real Life Strategies:
- Sex is meant to be sacramental, for the purpose of unifying a couple and for procreation.

- Make a clear plan on how to abstain. Talk about it with your friends and never discount the power of prayer.

- Great sex is not something you find through a casual one-night stand. It is only found in the safe walls of marriage where God, commitment, and family unite.

Real Life Wisdom:

We must do more than invoke the will of God if we wish to recover a viable Christian sexual morality.... Even if God's will is obvious, it cannot provide a rationale for any moral code until we are able to say, clearly and simply, how God's command speaks to us, how and why it addresses us not only as a demand but as good news.—Thomas E. Breidenthal

Savvy Resources for Additional Study:

Real Sex: The Naked Truth about Chastity
By Lauren Winner (Grand Rapids, MI: Brazos Press, 2005)

The Ethics of Sex
By Mark D. Jordan (London: Blackwell, 2001)

Christianity Today, "The Truth about Sex"
By Jenell Williams Paris (November 2001)